THE FINNS AND THE LAPPS

HOW THEY LIVE AND WORK

Volumes in the series:

The Finns
and the Lapps

HOW THEY LIVE AND WORK

John L. Irwin

PRAEGER PUBLISHERS
New York · Washington

BOOKS THAT MATTER

Published in the United States of America in 1973
by Praeger Publishers, Inc.
111 Fourth Avenue, New York, N.Y. 10003

Library of Congress Cataloging in Publication Data

Irwin, John L. 1942
THE FINNS AND THE LAPPS
(How they live and work)
SUMMARY: A cultural overview of Finland,
including discussions of the Finnish govern-
ment, economy, educational system, and
way of life, with special emphasis on the
unique life style of the Lapps.
    1.   Finland—Juvenile literature.   2.
Lapps—Juvenile   literature. [1. Finland
—Social life and customs. 2. Lapps]   1.
Title.
DK449.I78 1973   914.71'03'3   72-92885

Printed in Great Britain

Contents

List of Illustrations

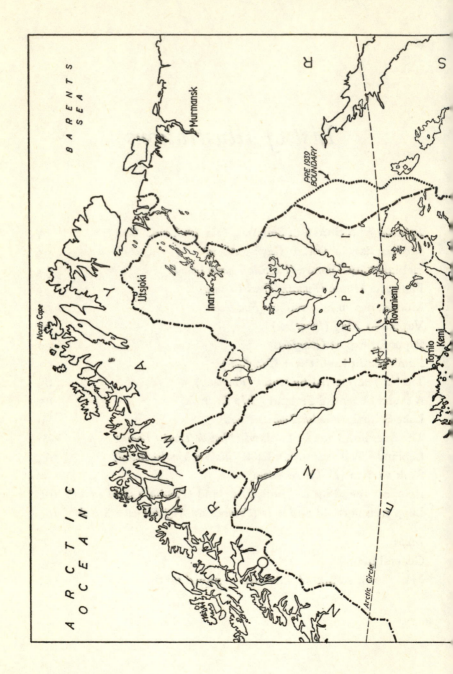

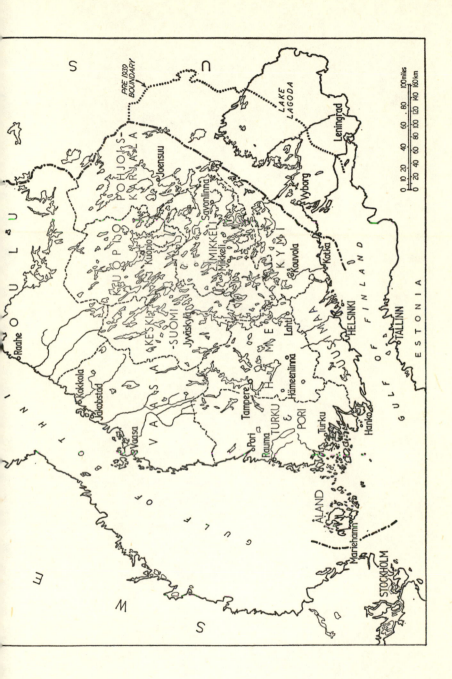

For Merja with love

Introduction

ALTHOUGH Finland was ruled by foreigners for many centuries
the Finns retained their own language, traditions and sense of
national identity. Since becoming independent in 1917 the
country has had to face a number of crises, internal and external, but in spite of difficulties has succeeded in surviving as a
nation state. In recent years Finland's economic development
has been considerable and today the majority of the population
enjoy an impressively high standard of living.

The position of the Lapp minorities in Finland, Norway and
Sweden has attracted considerable attention in recent years,
and a short section has therefore been included on the Lapps,
who at one time could be found in most areas of Finland.
Throughout the book the term 'Nordic countries' is used to
describe Finland, Norway, Sweden, Denmark and Iceland,
which conforms with the usual practice in these countries.

Note on exchange rates: During the period when this book was
being written exchange rates have fluctuated considerably,
making it difficult to convert Finnmarks into sterling and
dollars on a consistent pattern. Most of the conversions are
made at the rate which prevailed before December 1971, ie
£1 = 10.05 Fmks, $1 = 4.20 Fmks.

Note on place names: Many place names in Finland have a
Finnish and a Swedish form. In this book Finnish names are
used, with the exception of Åland (Ahvenanmaa) and its capital
Mariehamn (Maarianhamina).

11

I

The Country and the People

FINLAND is the northernmost state in Europe, reaching to within 1,370 miles of the North Pole and having about a third of its land area north of the Arctic Circle. It is a long narrow country, with a shape that resembles a man participating in a sack race, with one arm raised to keep his balance. Until 1944 there was another arm, which gave Finland access to the Arctic Ocean, but this was amputated by the Soviet Union following the Continuation War.

The proverbial crow flying from the extreme north of the province of Lappi (Finnish Lapland) would have to cover a distance of some 720 miles before it saw the islands in the Gulf of Finland that represent the southernmost extremity of the country. It would also have covered over 10 degrees of latitude, from 70°05′N to 59°30′N. A trip across Finland would prove less exhausting, the distance between the Gulf of Bothnia and the Russo-Finnish frontier being only 335 miles at the widest point. In addition to being a northern country, Finland is also on the eastern border of Europe—the 31°E line of longitude that passes through Karelia is east of Istanbul.

Although politically thought of as one of the smaller countries of Europe, Finland is, in terms of area, exceeded in size only by France, Spain and her immediate neighbours, Sweden and the Soviet Union. With an area of 130,094 square miles Finland is larger than the British Isles (121,600 square miles) and about half the size of the American state of Texas.

13

Finland has the distinction of being an 'emergent nation' in the literal sense, for ever since her release from the pressure of the great ice-sheets of the Quarternary Ice Age, approximately 10,000 years ago, the country has been rising from the sea. Land on the coast of Ostrobothnia is rising at the rate of some 3¼ft a century, though in the south the rate is only about a third of this. As one might expect, ice has been a dominant force in the formation of the Finnish landscape: the great outcrops of granite, morainic ridges like the Salpausselkä in southern Finland and the huge boulders, scattered like a giant's discarded marbles over the countryside, all bear witness to the constructive and destructive force of ice. Perhaps the most significant contribution made by glaciation to the Finnish landscape are the great hollows gouged in the rock, which have since filled with water to give Finland her extensive lake and river systems; these are estimated to account for between 9 and 10 per cent of the surface area of the country.

Finland tends to be a low-lying land, with the ground rising gradually from the coastal plains of the south and west towards the north-east. Only in Lapland are anything approaching mountains to be found, and even here the *tunturit*—or fells—are rarely over 1,500ft. Finland's highest point is Haltiatunturi on the frontier with Norway, which rises to 4,355ft. Although the average height of the country as a whole is less than 500ft above sea-level, it would not be true to say that Finland is flat. Constant faulting and uplift, together with the action of ice, have produced a rugged, broken landscape, which appears bleak and forbidding whenever it breaks through the mantle of forest that covers some 70 per cent of the land area. For centuries Finland has been a forest land, and even today wood is a raw material of great importance. In the south and west large areas have been cleared throughout history for cultivation or urban development, but in east and central Finland and far into Lapland the forest reigns supreme, broken only by lakes and rivers, the occasional settlement and even less frequent road.

Forestry apart, the most important agricultural area of Finland is the coastal plain stretching inland from the Gulf of Bothnia and the Gulf of Finland. Here much of the forest has been cleared and the fertile post-glacial soils, together with the longer growing season resulting from the modifying effect of the sea, mean that farms are larger and more prosperous and grow a greater variety of crops than those inland. The most productive area of the coastal plain is in the Turku-Loimaa region in the south-west. The farther north or east one goes from here the shorter the growing season becomes, while the period that livestock must be kept indoors becomes longer.

CLIMATE

Largely due to the benign influence of the Gulf Stream, Finland's climate is not as severe as that of other areas on the same latitude. During July Helsinki has a mean temperature of 64°F and it is not rare for temperatures to be in the seventies and eighties for considerable periods. In Finnish Lapland the July mean is 57°F (for Lapland see also p 142). February is the coldest month over the whole of Finland; the mean for Helsinki is 20°F and for Finnish Lapland 11°F, though lower temperatures, accompanied by freezing winds, can and do occur. Low temperatures are frequently accompanied by bright sunshine and blue skies and many a foolhardy foreigner has blithely stepped out into what he considers to be a beautiful spring day, only to find that the temperature is around −4°F. Precipitation in the form of rain and snow is heaviest in the south-west, 27in a year, compared with about 16in for Lapland.

During the winter, days are short: in the south during December the sun rises at about 9.30 am and sets just after 3 pm. Days get progressively shorter as one goes north, until at the 70th parallel there are fifty-one days of uninterrupted winter night. In compensation, summer days are long, with seventy-three days of continuous daylight in the far north.

Climatically, the most unpleasant time of year is autumn, when short, overcast days are accompanied by rain, sleet and snow, which changes rapidly into slush. The winter, in spite of the cold and the ice and snow, comes as a relief after the damp melancholy of autumn, and every chance is taken to exploit the opportunities for winter activities—as mentioned in Chapter 7. Winter naturally has a great effect on economic life, in particular on transport, as not only the lakes and river freeze but also the Baltic Sea.

The Finnish coastline stretches from the head of the Gulf of Bothnia to the Russian border east of Hamina in the Gulf of Finland. Although the length of the coastline is estimated to be about 700 miles, it is impossible to arrive at an accurate measurement as the coast is indented by a series of bays, peninsulas and creeks. In many places it is virtually impossible to establish where the coastline runs, as instead of terminating abruptly the mainland peters out into an intricate series of archipelagos. The largest of these is the Turku archipelago, which extends from Turku to Åland. It is made up of a multitude of small islands, ranging in size from small bare rocks, just large enough to support a warning light for shipping, to those which have a sizeable community, making their living from farming and fishing. The islands of the Turku, Vaasa, Hanko and Kotka archipelagos are extremely popular as sites for summer cottages, while the intricate waterways provide popular sailing and cruising grounds.

In addition to the sea coast, Finland shares frontiers with Sweden and Norway in the west and north, and with the Soviet Union to the east. The border with Sweden stretches from Tornio on the Gulf of Bothnia for 364 miles into Lapland, where a cairn marks the point where Finland, Norway and Sweden meet. The frontier with Norway continues from this point through 445 miles of northern Lapland, until once again three countries meet, this time Finland, Norway and the Soviet Union. The Russo-Finnish border runs south from Lapland for 788 miles to the Gulf of Finland.

RACIAL DERIVATION

The question of where the Finnish people originally came from is one that has fascinated the Finns for many years. None of the various theories put forward appears to be conclusive. In the nineteenth century in particular a number of scholars became involved in attempts to discover the origin of the Finnish nation. The best-known of these, M. A. Castrén, spent much time trying to prove that the Finns had originated in Central Asia and then gradually moved across Russia, until eventually they arrived at the Gulf of Bothnia where they made their home. Castrén, like many of the other researchers, relied a great deal on philological evidence, laying stress on the fact that Finnish belongs to the Finno-Ugrian language group. In essence it was suggested that the people who speak the languages belonging to this group once had a common homeland, which is thought to have been in the Urals. Critics of the theory claim that philological evidence is insufficient; the fact that nations speak languages belonging to the same group does not mean that the nations had the same point of origin.

The scholars who put forward the idea of the Central Asian homeland were not carrying out their research solely for scientific reasons. The period in which many of them were working corresponds to the time of an awakening of national feeling, when the Finns' main preoccupation was to prove that they were worthy to be considered a nation, with their own language, culture and ancestry. Not surprisingly, scientific detachment was to some extent overshadowed by patriotic enthusiasm. Present-day opinion inclines to the view that the Finns came from European Russia or the Baltic region, though the evidence is by no means conclusive in either case.

In the twelfth century Finland became a province of Sweden, but throughout the period of Swedish rule the Finns maintained their national identity and language. There was no large-scale migration of Swedes to Finland, though during prehistoric (ie before the Swedish conquest) and early historic times some Swedes settled in the south and west of the country and the islands off the Finnish coast. These Swedes retained their language and customs, and thus Finland has had from early times a Swedish-speaking minority.

LANGUAGE

Finland has two official languages, *suomi* (Finnish) and *svenska* (in Finnish *ruotsi*—Swedish). Finnish is the mother tongue of 92·4 per cent of the population, Swedish of 7·4 per cent. The Constitution of 1919 and a number of acts passed during the 1920s safeguard the rights of both Finnish and Swedish-speakers; thus Finnish citizens are entitled to use their mother tongue in courts of law and when dealing with the authorities, while the cultural and educational needs of both language groups are also provided for. The existence of two languages is seen in place names, too. Many towns, particularly in the south and west, have a Finnish and a Swedish name. Examples are, Helsinki: Helsingfors; Oulu: Uleåborg; and Turku: Åbo. If more than 10 per cent of the population of a commune speak the other national language the commune is regarded as bilingual. As the number of Finnish or Swedish-speakers in a commune is liable to change, the status of the communes is reviewed at regular intervals. At the end of 1972 the 512 communes in Finland were divided as follows: 427 Finnish-speaking, 12 bilingual (Finnish majority), 32 bilingual (Swedish majority), 41 Swedish-speaking. In addition to the official languages it is estimated that over 2,000 Lapps speak Lappish as their native tongue (see also p 155), while there are small groups speaking other languages, the largest of which is a Russian minority of about 2,500.

Finnish is, after Hungarian, the most widely spoken language of the Finno-Ugrian group. It is estimated that there are about 17 million people speaking languages belonging to this group. About 13 million of them are Hungarians, over 4 million are

Finns, while the Estonians (linguistically closest to the Finns) and the Moldavians both account for about a million people.

Finnish appears unfamiliar in both its written and spoken form to the average English-speaker. While in English the basic form of most words varies very little however they are used, the form of Finnish words changes according to context. Finnish is also a highly inflected language, depending on suffixes to express many of the meanings that are rendered by prepositions in English. Thus the word for house is *talo*, while 'in the house' is *talossa*, and 'from the house' *talosta*. In addition to meaning 'in the house' *talossa* can also mean 'in a house', as Finnish has no article, the meaning usually being made clear by the context. There are fifteen endings for Finnish nouns, some of them, though apparently the same, expressing different meanings. As an example, the word for table is *pöytä*; for *put* something 'on the table' the correct form is *pöydälle*, while for saying that something *is* 'on the table' the form is *pöydällä*. It will be noticed that the 't' in the basic form of the noun has changed to 'd' when the suffix is added, for consonant gradation is also characteristic of Finnish. This makes a foreigner's dictionary of questionable value at times, because it is not always possible to be sure what word should be looked up. The sign of the nominative plural is 't', which is added to a stem obtained by removing the 'n' of the genitive singular. Thus as the genitive of *kunta* (commune) is *kunnan*, the nominative plural is *kunnat* (in this case 't' becomes 'n' due to consonant gradation). A number of examples of words in the plural can be found elsewhere in this book.

As there are no silent letters in Finnish, one of the compounds of which the Finns are so fond can present a formidable challenge, for example 'a research assistant in the traffic planning department of the City Planning Office' is *kaupunkisuunnitteluviraston liikennesuunnitteluosaston tutkimusassistentti*. English uses thirteen words and a total of seventy-one letters, Finnish three words and seventy-two letters. Contact with other languages has meant the introduction of many loan-words, particularly in recent years as terms are required in specialist or scientific fields and for new inventions.

The origin of *Suomi*, the Finns' name for their country and language, remains obscure. It was originally applied only to the south-west, Varsinais-Suomi, and has only relatively recently been used for the whole country, which was previously known as *Itämaa*.

NATIONAL CHARACTERISTICS

It is difficult to make generalisations about a people, even when there are less than 5 million of them as in the case of the Finns. It is probably true to say that on the whole the Finns are withdrawn, frequently to the point of unfriendliness, and suspicious of strangers, whether foreigners or other Finns.

When talking about the Finns a distinction is frequently made between the inhabitants of the eastern part of the country, the *karjalaiset* (Karelians) and the *savolaiset* (those who live in the area known as Savo) and the people of central and western Finland. The easterners tend to be more light-hearted than their relatives further west, and are more inclined to be talkative and even boastful, though every now and again they lapse into a deep and often gloomy silence. The people of central Finland, the *hämäläiset*, are perhaps the most typical Finns, and they maintain a dour almost hostile outlook on life, preferring to watch the world rather than comment on it. Although the inhabitants of western Finland have much in common with the *hämäläiset*, proximity to the coast and the presence of the more gregarious Swedish speakers among them have produced a rather more outward-looking attitude. It is sometimes said that the true Finn only loses his reserve when he has a bottle in his hand and a considerable proportion of the contents of the bottle in his stomach. Although the per capita consumption of alcohol in Finland is lower than that in many southern countries, when the Finn drinks he drinks seriously. Once a bottle is open it is almost a point of honour to empty it.

Finns tend to have a great respect for authority, being prepared to accept with little question the rules and regulations imposed by the educational system, state or Church. Those in positions of authority, school-teachers, doctors, lawyers, civil servants and above all priests are treated with great respect, which is perhaps understandable in a country where education is regarded so highly. If, however, a Finn should suspect that he is being cheated of his rights, or being taken advantage of, he is likely to explode in a fit of anger which may even result in physical violence. It takes a great deal to move a Finn but, once moved, he or she is difficult to stop.

As far as physical characteristics are concerned, about 76 per cent of the men and 82 per cent of the women have fair hair, though the prevailing colour is light brown rather than blonde. The median height is 5ft 7in for men and 5ft 2in for women.

POPULATION

In 1950 the population of Finland was 4,029,800, in 1960 it was 4,446,200, while the census conducted at the end of 1970 arrived at a figure of 4,596,958. So, while the population was growing at a rate of 10·3 per cent during the fifties, in the sixties the rate dropped to 3·4 per cent. This was a lower rate of growth than was expected, for in 1960 it was estimated that the 1970 population would be 4,889,500.

As in other industrialised countries, Finland's birth rate has been falling since the beginning of the twentieth century. In the period 1931–5 it was 19·5 per 1,000, ie half that of fifty years earlier. There was a slight rise in the birth rate immediately after the war, for obvious reasons, but this has not been maintained, and in 1970 the figure was 13·7 per 1,000, compared with 16·2 per 1,000 for the United Kingdom and 18·2 per 1,000 for the United States. The death rate has also dropped since the beginning of the century, being 19·2 per 1,000 between 1901 and 1905 and 9·5 per 1,000 in 1970. As in Britain and the United States, the commonest causes of death are heart disease and cancer, though on average it is 65·4 years before men and 72·6 years before women succumb to these or other fatal diseases or accidents. But the Finn, particularly if he is a divorced, single or widowed male, is more likely to commit suicide than his counterpart in Britain or the USA. The suicide rate for Finland is 19·8 per 100,000, compared with 10·9 for the USA and 10·4 for the UK.

Every year between 35,000 and 40,000 marriages take place in Finland. During the sixties the average age for men contracting their first marriage was 25·1, for women 23. Between 1961 and 1969 the divorce rate rose from 0·88 per 1,000 of the population to 1·25 per cent per 1,000; the commonest cause of divorce was a breakdown of relations, this reason being given in 3,418 of the 5,895 divorces granted in 1969. At the end of the sixties the average number of children in a Finnish family was 2·3. In spite of the fact that more boys than girls are born in Finland—in 1970 out of 64,559 live births, 33,014 were boys—there are 1,072 women in Finland to every 1,000 men. This is partly explained by women's longer life expectancy (in 1968 there were 47,174 widowers in Finland compared with 235,458 widows) and also by the high male casualties during the war years 1939–45, during which it is estimated that some 110,000 men lost their lives.

Another reason why the population has not grown as fast as was anticipated during the sixties is that many Finns have emigrated to Sweden or elsewhere. It is impossible to find out exactly how many Finns are working in Sweden, as owing to the existence of a passport union and labour union there in no check on the movement of people between the Nordic countries. However, it is estimated that there is a Finnish minority of about 200,000 in Sweden and this does not include the 58,240 Finns who acquired Swedish nationality between 1948 and 1969. Most of the Finns living in Sweden are in the under-thirty-five age group, and many are highly trained, a loss in resources which has caused some alarm in Finland; both the state and industrial concerns are attempting to persuade skilled workers to return.

Between 1870 and 1914 about 258,000 Finns left to seek their fortunes in the New World, 90 per cent going to the United States and the remainder to Canada. Today there are large numbers of Americans of Finnish descent, living mainly in Minnesota, Michigan and other states of the north-west. Following World War I the number of emigrants going to America declined, but since World War II over 10,000 Finns have emigrated to Australia and New Zealand.

The density of population in Finland is 39·4 per square mile. The United Kingdom, with a population of 55,534,000, has a density of 589 per square mile, while the United States has 199,861,000 people and a population density of 56·3 per square mile. But the average figure for Finland is somewhat misleading, as in recent years there has been a large-scale migration from the never densely inhabited north to the south. In the north of Lapland there are only two persons per square mile, while in the south of Finland the figure rises to fifty. Another interesting trend is the movement from the country to towns. In the early years of the century only about 12·5 per cent of the population lived in urban areas, but by the beginning of 1972 55 per cent were living in towns.

Historically the area around Turku has always had considerable importance, as its name, Varsinais-Suomi (Finland Proper), implies. During the period when Finland was under Swedish rule Turku was the chief town of the province and the majority of the population lived in the south-west. Since the nineteenth century the emphasis has shifted eastwards towards the present capital, Helsinki, but the south maintains its dominant position. Helsinki, with a population of 520,425 in 1972 (11 per cent of the population of the country), is by far the largest city and, in addition to being the seat of government, is the commercial, industrial and cultural centre of the country. Some 25 per cent of the industry and 26 per cent of the industrial personnel of Finland are found in the Helsinki province of Uusimaa, which (apart from the rather special case of Åland) is the smallest of Finland's twelve provinces. At the beginning of 1972 the population of Finland was 4,638,090, 22 per cent of whom lived in Uusimaa, the majority of them in Helsinki,

Espoo (102,681) or Vantaa (90,706), which to a large extent act as dormitories for the capital.

Tampere (162,666) is Finland's second largest city and the Tampere economic area, Tammermaa, accounts for over 11 per cent of Finland's industry and about 13 per cent of the industrial workers. Turku is slightly smaller than Tampere, with 157,000 inhabitants, and the proportion of industry and industrial workers in Varsinais-Suomi is also less, being just over 10 per cent in both cases. The economic areas of Uusimaa, Tammermaa and Varsinais-Suomi, together with Etelä-Häme (South Häme) and Kaakkois-Suomi (South-East Finland) account for nearly 70 per cent of Finland's industry and industrial personnel. The total area of the four provinces containing these economic regions consists of about 25,810 square miles, 19·8 per cent of the land area of the country, and has 58 per cent of the population. By comparison the vast province of Lappi, with an area of 38,290 square miles, 29·5 per cent of the land area, has about 3·5 per cent of the country's industry, little more than 2 per cent of the industrial personnel and 4 per cent of the population. Other important urban centres are Lahti (91,161) about 60 miles north of Helsinki, Oulu (84,743) and Pori (76,942) both of which are on the west coast, and Kuopio (65,792) in eastern Finland. The centrally-situated town of Jyväskylä (59,469) should, according to some, be made the new capital of Finland, in order to shift the centre of gravity from the south of the country.

Another point to be taken into account when dealing with the relationship between Finland's population and land area is that in 1939 the country was somewhat larger than it is today. Before the war Finland's area was 147,761 square miles, but large areas in the south-east and north-east were surrendered to the Soviet Union as part of the peace terms following the Continuation War, making the present area of the country 130,094 square miles. In 1940 the population of Finland was about 3,695,000, some 425,000 of whom lived in the areas ceded to Russia. Following the Winter War virtually all of this population moved to Finland rather than remain under Soviet rule. When Finland regained much of the Karelian area during the Continuation War, about two-thirds of the displaced people moved back to their homes, only to leave in 1944 when Finland was once again defeated.

The problem of assimilating the Karelians into the larger population was a considerable one, particularly as economic conditions after the war were extremely difficult. However, the government adopted the policy that those who had not suffered directly as a result of the war should assist those who had; thus many of the Karelians who had lost their homes and farms were given land taken from landowners in the rest of Finland. Inevitably this caused a certain amount of friction, but it meant that to all intents and purposes the refugee problem was solved a few years after the war.

HISTORICAL LANDMARKS

A man cannot choose his relatives, or a country its neighbours. No small country would willingly be placed between two large powers; Finland's position between Sweden, representing the western cultural tradition, and Russia (or as it was earlier Novgorod and the Duchy of Moscovy) with an eastern culture, is of crucial importance for an understanding of her history.

Although there is evidence that Finland has been inhabited from about 8000 BC, information about the early cultures is far from complete, as already mentioned. It is thought that when the Finns arrived on the shores of the Gulf of Finland the interior of the area now named after them was inhabited by the Lapps, who supported themselves by hunting and trapping. Perhaps inhabited is the wrong word, as the population at that time must have been very small, and little or no conflict arose between the Lapps and the newcomers; there was room enough for all. According to the archaeological evidence the early inhabitants of Finland lived mainly on the coast, in the south and west, and supported themselves by hunting and fishing. Writing about AD 97 Tacitus describes a tribe called the 'Fenni' who 'are astonishingly wild and horribly poor'. The Fenni, according to the Roman historian, supported themselves by hunting and moved around from place to place, eating grass and sleeping on the ground. As the Finns' way of life was probably more developed at this time than that of the people described by Tacitus, it has been suggested that he was describing the Lapps. Many authorities, however, feel that the description is too generalised to apply to either Finns or Lapps and that Tacitus was merely repeating travellers' tales.

Before the coming of the Swedes in the middle of the twelfth century there was no administrative or political unity in Finland, and the inhabitants of the south-west found themselves in frequent conflict with the tribes living in Tasvastia (central Finland) and Karelia in the east. The Karelians tended to rely on the Novgorodians for military assistance, just as in peaceful times they looked upon them as trading partners. The western Finns had more contact with the Swedish trading centre of Birka, and later with the Germans based on the Baltic island of Gotland.

According to tradition, in 1157 King Erik of Sweden and the English-born Bishop of Uppsala led a crusade into Finland, the declared purpose of which was to baptise the heathen Finns. Whether King Erik was more interested in winning souls for a heavenly kingdom or territory for an earthly one is a matter for speculation, but as a result of the campaign Sweden gained a province, while shortly afterwards the Church gained a martyr and Finland a patron saint, when Henry of Uppsala was murdered by a Finnish farmer. Whatever the precise date of, and the reasons for, the Swedish expedition, by the next century Swedish influence had spread east, to where the castle of Viipuri, founded in 1293, marked the furthest extent of the kingdom of Sweden. In 1323 a frontier was agreed upon by the Swedes and the Novgorodians, but as in many places it ran through dense forest and unmapped wilderness it proved impossible to define with any precision and the border was long to remain a subject of contention.

Although Sweden had made Finland a province of the Swedish kingdom, providing a unity that had not existed before the invasion, the Swedes did not come as a conquering upper class as the Normans had done when they invaded England in 1066. The Finns had the same rights and privileges as other inhabitants of the kingdom, and were of course liable to the same taxes. From 1362 representatives from Finland participated in the election of the Swedish king, and Finns also sat in the *Riksdag* (parliament) in Stockholm from its earliest days. The Swedish crown established a number of castles in Finland, which acted as defensive strongpoints and administrative centres for the surrounding *linnanlääni* (castle county). The most important of these centres was Turku on the south-west coast, which with its castle, cathedral and proximity to Sweden was the obvious choice for the provincial capital. The other important town was Viipuri, which like Turku had trade links with Sweden and the Hanse cities. At first the main Finnish export was furs, joined later by forest products, mainly for naval use. The few other towns were usually on the coast. The majority of the population lived in small communities, supporting themselves by agriculture supplemented by hunting and fishing.

Finland was to remain united to Sweden for more than seven hundred years. One of the most important of the Swedish and western influences affecting the Finns was the Church, which in spite of its somewhat inauspicious beginnings soon became a considerable power in the land under the leadership of the Bishop of Turku. The association with Sweden also had a negative side, for Finland provided a buffer between Sweden proper and a frequently unfriendly east. In 1495, for example, when Sweden tried to secede from the Kalmar Union which in 1397 had united Denmark, Norway and Sweden-Finland under the Danish crown, Finland was invaded by the Russians, who were allied to the Danes. In 1523 after many years of bitter fighting —Turku was sacked by the Danes in 1509—Gustavus Vasa managed to break the hold of Denmark. His success was largely due to loans raised in the Hanse city of Lübeck, and in order to pay the merchants back he was forced to appropriate Church money, one result of which was Sweden's break with Rome in 1524.

The Reformation was to have far-reaching effects in Finland, for according to Lutheran teaching, brought from Germany by a number of Finnish churchmen who had studied in Wittenberg, all should have the opportunity to read the Bible, while the priest should expound the scriptures from the pulpit. Therefore priests in Finnish-speaking areas, that is the great majority, had to have a knowledge of Finnish. It is no accident that the leading figure of the Reformation in Finland, Mikael Agricola, who became Bishop of Turku in 1554, was the man who compiled the first Finnish grammar and translated the New Testament into Finnish.

Sweden's attainment of Great Power status in the seventeenth century was something of a mixed blessing for Finland, for expansion meant clashes with the Russians, frequently on Finnish soil or involving Finnish troops. During the Great Northern War the Swedish army withdrew completely from Finland between 1710 and 1713, leaving the Finns to fight a rearguard action during which the Russians occupied virtually the whole country. The Treaty of Nystad, which in 1721 stripped Sweden of her Baltic empire, also meant a revision of the borders of Finland, as Peter the Great was looking for security for his new capital of St Petersburg. Before long the map-makers were busy again, for following the war of 1741–3 further territory in the south-east was ceded to Russia.

It was this constant threat from Russia that persuaded a number of Finnish officers that, as there was little chance that the Finns could ever beat the Russians, the obvious course was to join them. Thus in 1788, when the autocratic Gustavus III declared war on Russia without consulting the *Riksdag*, a number of Finnish officers, together with Swedish sympathisers, formed the 'Anjala League', which proposed that Finland should secede from Sweden and become an 'independent' country under the protection of Russia. At this time the 'separatists', as they were called, were few in number and the king had little difficulty in suppressing them. However, some twenty years later, following another Russo-Swedish conflict, Finland did become part of the Russian Empire by the Treaty of Hamina (Fredrickshamn), 1809. Earlier in the year, at the Diet of Porvoo (Borgå), Tsar Alexander I had promised the Finnish Estates that as Grand Duke he would respect the institutions that had been established during Swedish times. Thus when Finland came under Russian rule she retained her civil service—staffed by Finns and free from Russian interference— army, legal system and post office, while the Lutheran Church was recognised as the official Church. In many respects Finland became a constitutional monarchy—its Diet began to meet regularly in the latter decades of the century—on the fringes of an autocratic empire.

For ninety years successive tsars tended to leave Finland alone, and the majority of Finns seemed content with their position. However, as in other countries of Europe, the nineteenth century was a period of national awakening. Although Finland had been ruled by the Swedish crown for seven centuries the Finns had never been fully integrated into the Swedish nation. One reason for this was the physical separation imposed by the Gulf of Bothnia, but far more important was the fact that the Finns had retained their own language. It is estimated that in 1809 Swedish, the official language of the Grand Duchy, was the mother tongue of a mere 15 per cent of the population, and so it is hardly surprising that one of the first aims of the early nationalist movement was to improve the status of Finnish.

The leading figure in the language struggle was Johan Vilhelm Snellman, whose thesis was that language is the distinguishing characteristic of a nation and therefore, if Finland was to aspire to nationhood, Finnish must be the language of education and administration. Interest in the language question was fostered by the publication, in 1835, of the *Kalevala*, a collection of ancient runes and songs, compiled and edited by Elias Lönnrot to form a continuous poem describing the origin of the Finnish people in heroic terms. The *Kalevala* had a great effect on the nationalist movement, as did the writings of other patriots, notably the poet J. L. Runeberg and the novelist and historian Zachris Topelius. Although both Runeberg and Topelius, like many others involved in the movement, wrote in Swedish, their sentiments were distinctly Finnish and had great influence. In spite of resistance from the—Swedish-speaking— civil service, Snellman and his friends eventually achieved their primary aim when in 1863 a language decree was published, putting Finnish on an equal footing with Swedish in administrative offices and courts of law.

In its early years Finnish nationalism tended to be of interest to a small, rather exclusive group of educated men and women, and had little appeal to the majority of the population. In February 1899, however, the nationalist cause received a boost from an unexpected quarter. Nicholas II illustrated the fact that Finland's constitutional monarchy depended on the whim of the tsar by publishing a proclamation increasing the powers of the Russian government to intervene in Finnish affairs. As the 'February Manifesto' was held by the Finns to run counter to the provisions of Porvoo, a petition, signed by the majority of the adult population, was sent to St Petersburg protesting at the tsar's action. He refused to accept it, and a second one, signed by distinguished figures from all over Europe, fared no better.

In 1906, following a revolution in Russia and a general strike in Finland, the tsar made concessions and Finland was given a new and more liberal constitution. The respite did not continue, and the years before World War I were marked by the struggle of the Finns to retain what they considered to be their rights. Their chance finally came in 1917 when the monarchy in Russia was overthrown. On 6 December 1917 Finland declared her independence, and this was recognised by the Bolshevik government at the end of the month. Before the newly independent nation could establish itself, however, the question of who should rule had to be settled, a process that was to involve a short, but extremely bloody, civil war.

The 'Reds' were attempting to establish a socialist state on the Russian model, but the 'Whites' felt that this would inevitably mean Finland's reabsorption into Russia, particularly as the 'Reds' had the assistance of some of the Russian troops stationed in Finland. For their part the 'Whites' were aided by German troops and a cadre of Finns who had been trained in Germany—the 27th Jäger battalion. German aid was accepted with great reluctance by the 'White' commander-in-chief, Carl Gustav Mannerheim, a former tsarist general, who felt that what he regarded as a war for Finnish independence could and should be won by the Finns themselves. The war lasted for only five months, between January and May 1918, but some of the wounds it inflicted are still felt. In addition to the numbers killed on both sides during the fighting, many factory officials, landowners and priests were tortured and murdered by the 'Reds', while many 'Reds' were executed without trial or died of hunger or disease in 'White' prison camps. Following the war relations with the Soviet Union remained strained until the Treaty of Dorpat, 1920, which acknowledged the right of Finland to exist as a separate nation.

Finland then found herself in dispute with another neighbour, Sweden, over the ownership of the Swedish-speaking Åland islands. The Åland question was settled amicably in 1921, following arbitration by the League of Nations, though the position of Swedish-speakers on the mainland (about 11 per cent of the population in 1920) remained difficult, leading at times to physical violence. Another cause of friction during the inter-war period, not entirely separate from the language question, was the rise of right-wing groups aggressively dedicated to the service of a Finnish Finland and the destruction of communist and socialist groups. Many Finns were convinced during the 1920s that the communists, under the direction of Moscow, were planning a coup in Finland, and the communist parades and meetings did little to allay these fears. In 1930 the right-wing Lapua Movement (*Lapuan Liike*), which had been conducting an intimidation campaign against the left-wing parties, succeeded in getting the Communist Party banned. Inspired by this success they then attempted to take over the government, but were prevented by the firm action of President

Svinhufvud and the army who, unlike the authorities in some other European countries at this time, were not prepared, in the last resort, to compromise with the extreme right wing. The political struggles did much to keep the memories of 1918 alive, and it was not until the outbreak of the Winter War, when virtually all Finns united in face of the Russian threat, that many (but by no means all) of the ghosts of the civil war were laid.

In 1938 the Russians proposed that discussions should be held with a view to revising the Russo-Finnish frontier in the south-east in order to safeguard Leningrad. The Finns, however, refused to discuss the Russian suggestions. The following year the USSR entered into treaties with the Baltic states of Latvia, Lithuania and Estonia, and in October repeated their proposals to Finland. In spite of the advice of a number of prominent people, including General Mannerheim, at this time chairman of the defence committee, that concessions should be made, the Finnish government refused to give way, and on 30 November 1939 the Russians attacked Finland. The Soviet Union had obviously expected an easy victory over the ill-prepared Finns, for they had been led to believe that the Finnish proletariat was eagerly awaiting a renewal of the con-

———

Lakeuden Risti church in Seinäjoki, designed by Alvar Aalto

Modern flats in Turku

flict of 1918. But the Finns united, and this national solidarity, combined with the fighting quality of the Finnish army and one of the severest winters experienced in the north, halted the Red Army advance. During the winter of 1939–40 the Finns won the admiration and moral support of much of the world for their stand, but the support did not manifest itself in terms of physical aid (the British and French governments discussed sending an expeditionary force to Finland but, perhaps fortunately for everybody, the plan was not put into effect) and the Finnish leaders realised that they would have to give way. By the Treaty of Moscow, 12 March 1940, the Russians secured the territory they wanted and much more, including Viipuri, Finland's second largest city.

The arguments about the Winter War should fill a number of books and indeed have done so—few topics in Finnish history have been discussed at such length. Most Finns seem to believe that if they had not stood firm in 1939 they would have shared the fate of the Baltic states, which were in 1940 incorporated into the Soviet Union. This does not necessarily follow, however, for whereas the Baltic states lay between Russia and Germany, Finland is, strategically speaking, on the fringes of Europe. It is true that during the Continuation War, which

Helsinki City Theatre, designed by Timo Penttilä and completed in 1967

Finlandia House, designed by Alvar Aalto, opened in December 1971 began in June 1941, German troops fought alongside the Finns, but they were co-belligerents, not allies. The unwillingness of the Finnish commander-in-chief, Mannerheim, to attack Leningrad in support of the Germans who were attacking from the south, meant that the Finnish front was little more than a sideshow to the war as a whole. Although between 1941 and 1944 the Finns briefly regained the land they had lost in 1940, they were unable to hold it and the Continuation War also ended in defeat in September 1944.

The peace terms of 1944 (which were confirmed by the Treaty of Paris in 1947) were far harsher than those of 1940. In addition to reaffirming the borders of 1940, the Russians took the Petsamo corridor, with its nickel mines and access to the Arctic. Hanko, the naval base the Russians had secured in 1940, was handed back, but in its place they took Porkkala near Helsinki, on a fifty-year lease (it was in fact returned in 1955). Extreme right-wing organisations were banned and the Communist Party was legalised, while those held to be 'responsible' for the war were brought to trial. War reparations amounting to $300 million (£75 million) were imposed, to be paid off over a period of six years (see also p 80). Finally, as if the Finns had not had enough of war, they had to drive the remaining German forces out of Lapland, an operation which took several months of bitter fighting, during which the Germans destroyed many villages and towns in Finnish Lapland.

FINNISH NEUTRALITY SINCE THE WAR

The president at the end of the war had been Marshal Mannerheim, but in 1946 he resigned on grounds of ill-health and was succeeded by Dr J. K. Paasikivi. It was under Paasikivi that the basic direction of Finnish foreign policy was established—the 'Paasikivi line'—the aim of which is to ensure Finnish independence while maintaining good relations with the Soviet Union. In 1948 the Russo-Finnish Mutual Assistance Pact was signed, according to which, 'In the eventuality of

Finland, or the Soviet Union through Finnish territory, becoming the object of an armed attack by Germany or any state allied with the latter, Finland will . . . fight to repel the attack . . . if necessary, with the assistance of, or jointly with, the Soviet Union.' The Pact also states that neither party may join an alliance 'directed against the other' and provides for discussions in the event of a 'threat of an armed attack'.

It is the existence of the 1948 Pact (which was renewed in 1955 and again in 1970) that has made it difficult for many, especially in the West, to accept Finland's description of herself as a neutral country. They argue that the Pact gives the Soviet Union a great deal of power to interfere in Finnish foreign affairs and that the terms of the Pact align Finland with the Soviet Union against the West. Many western politicians also feel that the USSR plays too great a part in Finland's internal affairs; during the sixties the term 'Finlandisation' was coined to describe a country whose affairs are conducted under the supervision of another power. A large number of Finns would share the view that the Russians take too much interest in Finnish domestic politics, and it is often claimed that governments and even presidents must be chosen with an eye on Moscow. The continual protestations of neutrality in the Finnish press and the mouths of Finnish politicians may sound like a lady of doubtful reputation proclaiming her virginity—if there is no doubt about the matter why keep referring to it? However, for most Finns neutrality does not mean complete freedom from international agreements, but rather non-involvement in the East-West line-up in Europe. Thus Finland has an agreement with the Soviet Union for a specific purpose and with the aim of safeguarding her own security. Finland is not part of the Warsaw Pact, nor of course, of NATO.

Although most Finns would probably prefer Finland's neutrality to be like Sweden's, they realise that the facts of geography are even less favourable to them than to the Swedes. No matter how long they close their eyes the Soviet Union will not go away, so they prefer to keep their eyes open and follow the policy which seems to be most advantageous for Finland.

They are quick to point out that theirs is the only European country sharing a frontier of any length with the Soviet Union that has not succumbed to communist rule. The reason for this is of great interest and has been discussed at length, both inside and outside Finland. There seems little doubt that from the Russian point of view an independent Finland that is willing to discuss matters of mutual importance with the USSR is infinitely preferable to a Finland that is a reluctant member of the communist camp. A Soviet-controlled Finland might well have driven Sweden into the arms of NATO and greatly increased tension in northern Europe. In addition the Finns gave the Russians ample evidence between 1939 and 1944 that a takeover would not have been easy.

Since 1956 the direction of foreign policy has been the responsibility of President Urho Kekkonen, who has followed in his predecessor's footsteps so closely that the 'Paasikivi line' has been renamed the 'Paasikivi-Kekkonen line'. Recently, however, there have been signs that a new and independent 'Kekkonen line' has been developing, more active than that of the fifties and early sixties. One of the first manifestations of the new line was Finland's success in becoming joint host, with Vienna, to the Russo-American Strategic Arms Limitation Talks (SALT). The Finns were also delighted when delegates to the European Security Conference assembled in the conference centre at Otaniemi just outside Helsinki for preliminary talks in autumn 1972. Finland's role as an 'honest host' is not, of course, entirely disinterested: although their desire for world peace is genuine enough, the Finns know that the publicity of a major international gathering would be to their benefit. Another step towards a more active foreign policy was Finland's announcement in November 1972 of her intention to establish full diplomatic links with both East and West Germany.

Finland's position as regards the European Economic Community is somewhat ambiguous. Although Finnish politicians have stated that it would be impossible for Finland to join, many of her main trading partners are members. During 1972 a trade agreement was negotiated between Finland and the

EEC, but largely owing to the attitude of the Social Democratic Party its ratification was delayed for further discussions on the question of price controls. The attempt of Max Jakobson to become Secretary General of the United Nations can also be seen in the light of Finland's active foreign policy line. Ever since Finland joined the UN in 1955 she has been an active member, and many Finns had hoped that their reward would be in the form of the Secretary General's chair.

2

How the Country is Run

ALTHOUGH Finland was a monarchy for many centuries, first under Swedish and later under Russian rule, there has never been, strictly speaking, a King of Finland. Shortly after the achievement of independence, however, the victors in the Civil War invited Prince Friedrich Karl of Hesse, brother-in-law of the Kaiser, to accept the Finnish crown; but although Friedrich Karl prepared himself by spending the summer of 1918 studying Finnish, the prospects of Germany's defeat, coupled with opposition to the idea of a monarchy, meant that he never ascended the throne. In 1919 the Constitution of independent Finland declared the country a republic, and in July of that year Professor K. J. Ståhlberg was elected president. Of the seven presidents since Ståhlberg, the longest-serving has been Dr Urho Kekkonen, who was first elected in 1956, his third term of office expiring in 1974.

Presidential elections take place every six years and, as in the United States, the president is chosen by an electoral college, numbering 300, whose members have been chosen by all adult citizens. Although as in the USA the presidential election is conducted along party lines, the Finnish president, once in office, is expected to renounce all party ties and affiliations. He does not, however, become a non-political figurehead; on the contrary he has far-reaching powers and takes an active part in both domestic and foreign affairs. The president can initiate legislation and is also responsible for approving bills passed by parliament, though his veto is only suspensive, not absolute. He summons and can dissolve parliament, and is responsible for the selection of the prime minister and other cabinet ministers, not to mention a large number of public officials including bishops and certain university professors. Although legislation is the responsibility of parliament, the president is permitted to issue statutory orders, providing that these do not conflict with the law of the country. The president's most important role is in foreign policy, where he is given a virtually free hand, though treaties and issues of war and peace must have the assent of parliament. It is this freedom of action in foreign affairs, reminiscent of the royal autocracy of earlier times, together with the length of President Kekkonen's period of office, that has led cynics to suggest that Finland is the only republic with a king.

There is no provision for a vice-president in the Finnish system, so that the most important figure after the president is the prime minister (*pääministeri*), who is head of the government and chairman of the Council of State or cabinet (*valtioneuvosto*). Whereas in Britain a minister must be a member of one or other of the Houses of Parliament, a Finnish minister, like his American counterpart, does not need to sit in the one-chamber parliament or *eduskunta*. A minister who does not have a seat in the *eduskunta* can speak in debates but is not permitted to vote. There are usually sixteen or seventeen ministers in a Finnish government, all of whom sit in the *valtioneuvosto*.

For most of the period of Russian rule Finland retained the Diet of the Four Estates that had been established in Swedish times. In 1906, however, the constitution was reformed and the old diet was replaced by a unicameral parliament, elected by the entire adult population of the country. Thus almost overnight the electorate increased from 125,000 to 1,125,000 and Finland became the first European country to give women the vote in parliamentary elections. Although modifications have been made to the Finnish parliamentary system since independence, today's *eduskunta* is basically the same as that established in 1906. It consists of 200 representatives (*kansanedustaja*) who are elected by a complex system of proportional representation. The parliamentary term lasts for four years and general elections are usually held on fixed days: the third Sunday and Monday in March.

Proportional representation in the January 1972 election brought eight parties to the *eduskunta*; while the existence of this system of voting has meant that since independence Finland has never had a one-party majority government. Indeed, almost half the cabinets since 1917 have not had a majority backing in the *eduskunta*, though the opposition parties have usually been so disorganised themselves that the government has been able to continue. Even so, since World War II the average period of office has been only just over twelve months. The resignation of a government does not necessarily mean new elections, as the president will try to form a government from among the sitting members of the *eduskunta*, augmented by outsiders if necessary. If this proves impossible he can form a caretaker administration of experts. The powers of intervention available to the president are considerable, but nevertheless there is a strong tradition of parliamentarianism in Finland, which means that whenever possible governments must enjoy parliamentary support. Caretaker administrations, such as those of 1970 and 1972, are regarded as stop-gaps and are intended to hold office for only a limited period.

The *eduskunta* assembles in February each year and sits for a total of 120 days, usually divided into a spring and an autumn term. The first duty of the representatives is to elect a Speaker (*puhemies*) from among their number, and he holds the post for the parliamentary year. Then a number of committees are appointed for preparing and considering legislation. The most important is the *suuri valiokunta* (Grand Committee), consisting of forty-five members, which is designed to exercise some of the powers of a second chamber. Other standing committees include the Constitutional Committee, the Legislative Committee and the Foreign Affairs Committee, all with seventeen members, the Finance Committee, with not less than twenty-one members and the Bank Committee (which has responsibility for the Bank of Finland) with about eleven members. Ministers are not permitted to be members of these bodies, but with the consent of the appropriate committee they can attend meetings and participate in discussions. The committee system has considerable importance, for it is at the committee stage that legislation is examined in detail before it goes back to the *eduskunta* for a vote.

Although either the government or individual representatives can initiate legislation, in practice most bills are introduced by the government. Following the admittance of a bill and its debate on the first reading, it is referred to the *suuri valiokunta*. Here a report is prepared which is then debated in the second reading. If the report is accepted the second reading is concluded, though in the event of disagreement the bill returns to the *suuri valiokunta* for amendment. If agreement is reached and the bill is accepted by the *eduskunta* the second reading is concluded. The third reading comes when the *eduskunta* decides to accept or reject the bill as it stands; no amendments can be introduced at this stage. The issue is usually resolved at the third reading, but with the agreement of a third of the representatives a final decision can be deferred until new elections have been held.

POLITICAL PARTIES

The first political parties recognisable as such in modern Finland were the Swedish and Finnish parties formed at the end of the nineteenth century as a result of the language question. In 1899 the Social Democratic Party (*Sosiaalidemokraattinen-puolue/SDP*) was founded, but had little influence until after the parliamentary reforms of 1906, when it became the largest party in the Diet. The Agrarian Union (*Maalaisliitto*) which was established in 1908 drew much of its support from rural areas, though in 1965 it sought to enlarge its appeal by changing its name to the Centre Party (*Keskustapuolue/Kepu*). The Finnish 'Conservative Party', the National Coalition Party (*Kansallinen Kokoomuspuolue/KoK*) was formed after the Civil War, and the Liberal People's Party (*Liberaalinen Kansan Puolue/LKP*) also originated at this time in the form of the Progressive Party. The

Finnish Communist Party (*Suomen Kommunistinen Puolue*) was founded in the Soviet Union in 1918 by left-wingers who had fled there after the Civil War. It was banned in 1930 but legalised by the 1944 peace treaty, and since the war has succeeded in attracting a considerable proportion of the national vote as a member of the Finnish People's Democratic League (*Suomen Kansan Demokraattinen Liitto/SKDL*). The Swedish Party is still represented in the *eduskunta* by the Swedish People's Party (*Svenska Folk Partiet/SFP*) while other parties are the Finnish Rural Party (*Suomen Maaseudun Puolue/SMP*), which split off from the Centre Party in 1966, and the Christian League (*Suomen Kristillinen Liitto/SKL*).

Virtually every general election in Finland is followed by a period of horse-trading during which the various parties look around for potential allies in forming a government. Loosely speaking there is a division between the *sosialistit* (socialists) and *ei-sosialistit* (non-socialists), though in practice the parties often find it inexpedient to combine with those who might appear to be their natural allies, and a deadlock lasting for weeks or even months can result. Since World War II the largest groups in the *eduskunta* have been the Agrarian/Centre Party, the Social Democrats and the SKDL, and the first government after the war was a coalition containing members of all three. In 1948, however, the agreement came to an end, and for the next decade and into the sixties the government was in the hands of an Agarian-Social Democratic coalition, assisted by members of the Liberal and Swedish parties. In the mid-1960s SKDL ministers were again included in the coalition, though on a number of occasions they found co-operation difficult.

In the general election of March 1970, Kepu, the SDP and the SKDL all lost seats, the main beneficiaries being the rightwing parties, *Kokoomus* and the SMP (the latter which had held only a single seat in the 1966–70 parliament increased its representation to 18, largely by appealing to 'the silent majority' in the depressed agricultural areas of Finland). Although a number of attempts were made to form a parliamentary government no progress was made, and in May the Lord Mayor of

Helsinki, Teuvo Aura, was asked by President Kekkonen to form a caretaker administration. Two months later Dr Ahti Karjalainen, who had been foreign minister before the 1970 election, succeeded in forming a cabinet, made up of ministers from Kepu, SDP, SKDL, SFP and LKP. In March 1971 the SKDL ministers left the government, and a reconstituted Karjalainen administration continued until autumn 1971, when it ran into difficulties over agricultural policy. The president accepted Dr Karjalainen's resignation and announced a new general election for January 1972; in the meantime Aura returned as prime minister. After the election of January 1972 the distribution of seats in the *eduskunta* was: SDP: 55, SKDL: 37, Kepu: 35, KoK: 34, SMP: 18, SFP: 10, LKP: 7, SKL: 4. Once again there were protracted negotiations and at the end of February a minority Social Democrat government was formed, under the leadership of Mr Rafael Paasio. In July 1972 Paasio resigned on the grounds that a minority government could not take the responsibility of signing a trade agreement with the EEC. At the end of August Mr Kalevi Sorsa, who had been foreign minister in the Paasio administration, formed a coalition consisting of Social Democrats, the Centre Party, the Liberal Party and the Swedish People's Party.

THE CHANCELLOR OF JUSTICE AND THE PARLIAMENTARY OMBUDSMAN

Sweden appointed the world's first Ombudsman and it was not until 1919, when the Finnish constitution made provision for such an official, that any country followed her example. Much earlier, however, in 1812, a Procurator or Chancellor of Justice, who had direct access to the tsar, had been appointed with the task of supervising the work of government officials and the Senate in the Grand Duchy of Finland.

Today the Parliamentary Ombudsman (*Eduskunnan oikeus-asiamies/OA*) and the Chancellor of Justice (*Oikeuskansleri*) complement each other. The Chancellor of Justice is appointed by the president and is responsible for supervising the working of the government and also judges in courts of law. As legal adviser to the government the *oikeuskansleri* also carries out the duties of attorney-general. The Ombudsman is elected by the *eduskunta* and is responsible to that body, though he cannot be a *kansanedustaja* himself. His term of office is four years, and during this time he cannot be dismissed, though the *eduskunta* may refuse to elect him for another term. Whereas the *oikeuskansleri* is responsible for seeing that ministers and the president obey the law, the OA supervises the civil service, the police, the law courts and the armed forces. He can visit all the institutions under his jurisdiction—his terms of reference specifically include prisons—and convicts and inmates of mental hospitals share the right of the general public to communicate directly with his office. Although the OA has the right to institute proceedings against a civil servant who has made an unjustified decision, his usual course of action would be to send a reminder to the official in question, and only take action if the reminder is ignored.

LOCAL GOVERNMENT

Modern Finland is divided into twelve administrative provinces (*läänit*), each one headed by a governor (*maaherra*), who is appointed by the president on the advice of the *valtioneuvosto*. Administration within each province is carried out by the provincial board (*lääninhallitus*), which acts as the guardian of state interests within the area. The provincial board nominates the more important members of the provincial government, such as the counsellor (*lääninneuvos*) and the treasurer (*taloudenhoitaja*), though the actual appointment is made by the *valtioneuvosto*. The Finnish provinces are in no way comparable with states in the USA or even counties in the United Kingdom, because they are not run by an elected body but are administrative units; local government functions proper are carried out by the communes.

The smallest province, that of Åland (Ahvenanmaa in Finnish), which consists of a group of islands between Finland and Sweden, has a rather special status. In 1921 a decision of the League of Nations confirmed that the islands belonged to Finland on the basis of historical ownership, even though the overwhelming majority of the population spoke Swedish and voted in a plebiscite to join Sweden. By the Government of Åland Act, 1951 the province was given a considerable measure of self-government. Swedish is the language of administration and education and it is virtually impossible to find signs in Finnish in the capital Mariehamn, except in places like coffee-bars. Male citizens of Åland are not liable to conscription, nor does Finland maintain military installations on the islands.

There are three different kinds of commune in Finland: the rural commune (*maalaiskunta*), the borough or 'market town' (*kauppala*) and the town or city (*kaupunki*). The classification of communities into these categories depends largely on size, though in some cases an ancient *kaupunki* might be smaller than a neighbouring *kauppala* of more recent foundation. Each commune provides a variety of services for its inhabitants, and the higher the status of the commune the greater the control over these services. Some *maalaiskunnat* have combined forces in order to provide certain specialised services such as hospitals, and the increasing number of these 'joint communes' has led to discussions about the reform of local government, so that powers taken away from the provinces might be given to an intermediate body.

The council of each commune is elected by the citizens, and it is the duty of anyone who is nominated to stand for election and serve, unless he or she has a genuine reason such as age, illness or frequent absence from the commune, for not doing so. The number of councillors ranges from thirteen to seventy-seven, depending on the size of the population. In rural communes the central administrative board for the commune is elected by the council members and consists of a chairman, who sits for four years (though many places now have a fulltime commune manager—*kunnanjohtaja*) and ordinary members who sit for two years. In both classes of towns a fulltime manager (*kaupunginjohtaja* or *kauppalanjohtaja*) acts as chairman of the municipal board, along with at least four councillors who are elected annually. It is the ambition of every commune to be promoted to the next highest status, and every year the *valtioneuvosto* considers applications from *maalaiskunnat* wishing to become *kauppalat* and *kauppalat* wishing to become *kaupungit*. The change of status takes place officially at midnight on 31 December, and is accompanied by speeches, fireworks and other festivities. In 1972 Finland had 55 towns, 27 boroughs and 430 rural communes.

THE LEGAL SYSTEM

Many of the basic features of the Finnish legal system date from Swedish times, and some areas of law are still covered by the General Code of 1734. During the nineteenth century a number of reforms were introduced, but in many cases these too followed the Swedish example. From 1919 onwards Finland has participated in discussions with Sweden, Denmark and Norway on legislation, which has increased the Scandinavian element in Finnish law. Court procedure and the training of lawyers are also closely related to the practice in other Nordic countries.

In rural areas a professional judge sits in a district court (*kihlakunnanoikeus*), together with a jury (*lautakunta*) of between five and twelve members. Although composed of ordinary citizens, like the British and American juries, the Finnish jury differs from them in a number of important respects. In the first place the Finnish jury serves for a longer period, while secondly it has the responsibility of deciding questions of law and fact. Thirdly the Finnish jury decides on the verdict in consultation with the judge. Only a unanimous decision by the jury can overrule the judge. If the judge dissents, and is supported by any of the jurors, this is the decision which is accepted as the verdict. In older urban areas the court of first instance is the town court (*raastuvanoikeus*) consisting of three judges, and here verdicts are given in accordance with the majority decision. The judges in such a court are nearly always professionals, but in small towns the junior members of the court are not required to be lawyers.

For the purposes of appealing against sentence or judgement in the lower courts, the country is divided into four areas, each one having an appeal court (*hovioikeus*); this court also acts as a court of first instance in serious criminal cases. The president of the appeal court and his two colleagues are all professional judges, as are the members of the Supreme Court (*Korkein Oikeus*) in Helsinki. The quorum for the Supreme Court is usually five, though it may be increased at the discretion of the Chief Justice. Normally the Supreme Court is the highest court of appeal, but in certain circumstances the President of the Republic has the power to grant a pardon.

There is no distinction in Finland between criminal and civil courts; criminal hearings, divorce proceedings and claims for damages are all heard in the same court. There are no preliminary hearings, as in Britain and the United States, and this means that proceedings tend to take some time, particularly as the court procedure is very thorough.

A man or woman who wishes to practise as a lawyer in Finland must first of all have a degree in law from a Finnish university. Upon graduation a decision must be made between the bench and the bar, for the judiciary is a career in itself, in contrast to Britain, where appointment to the bench is looked upon as the successful culmination of a career as a barrister. Another difference between Finnish and British practice is that there is no distinction between solicitors and barristers; thus the Finnish *asianajaja* is a lawyer in the American sense. A lawyer who wishes to serve on the bench begins his service in the district court, and if successful is then promoted. Those who wish to have a career at the bar spend three years getting practical experience in the courts, after which they can apply for membership of the Finnish Bar Association (*Suomen Asianajajaliitto*), which acts as the supervisory body for Finnish lawyers.

The chief public prosecutor is the Chancellor of Justice

(p 45), though he usually delegates his authority in the lower courts. Each province has a regional official who acts as head of the local rural prosecutors, the chief inspecting constable (*poliisitarkastaja*), who appears in the courts in person only in serious criminal cases. The local prosecutor in rural areas is the sheriff (*nimismies*), who is also the head of a rural police district. In urban areas there is a town prosecutor (*kaupunginviskaali*).

THE POLICE

The Finnish police force is a national body controlled by the Minister for Internal Affairs. In each province the *poliisitarkastaja* (see above) is the senior police officer and he supervises the sheriffs who act as chiefs of police in rural areas. In towns the police are under the control of a police commissioner (*poliisimestari*). The mobile police (*liikkuva poliisi*) and the central criminal police (*keskusrikospoliisi*) are both controlled from Helsinki, though they co-operate with the local police offices when necessary. Although police officers are permitted to carry firearms, their use is strictly controlled by law. In March 1971 a number of towns introduced traffic wardens—popularly known as *lappuliisat*—to supervise parking meters.

———

Modern design in ceramics

Vappu—1 May

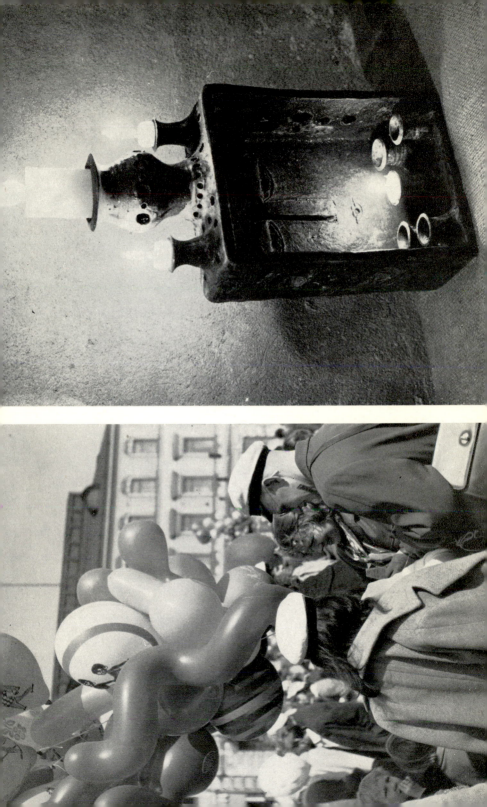

THE PENAL SYSTEM

About 90 per cent of all cases are settled by payment of a fine. So far as those miscreants who do go to prison are concerned, about 80 per cent of them at any one time are housed in closed institutions. Since 1946 a number of labour camps (*työsiirtolat*) have been established for first offenders convicted of less serious crimes. These seem to have had considerable success, largely because they do not encourage anti-social tendencies among the inmates. Offenders serving sentences in these labour camps wear their own clothes and work in industrial plants near by, being paid a regular wage which is used to help their families. Prison camps (*vankisiirtolat*) resemble labour colonies, apart from the fact that their inmates have already served part of their sentence in a closed prison (*vankila*).

The Finns believe that there is a strong correlation between drinking and traffic accidents and accordingly take strong action against anyone who has been drinking before taking charge of a motor vehicle. The relation between drinking and offences is not confined to driving, however, for statistics show

———

Paper and allied products still account for nearly 40 per cent of Finnish exports . . .

. . . but other products, such as this ice-breaker built in Finland for the Swedish state, are becoming increasingly important

D

that a considerable proportion of crimes in Finland, particularly those involving offences against the person, such as man-slaughter or wounding, are committed under the influence of alcohol.

The age of criminal responsibility is fifteen and children under this age are the responsibility of the child welfare boards. Over the age of fifteen children are tried in the adult courts, as there is no special system for juveniles: there are however special institutions for young offenders.

CURRENCY AND TAXATION

Finland has had her own currency and monetary system since 1860. The basic currency unit is the *markka* which is divided into 100 *penniä*. At the present time there are six coins, 1, 5, 10, 20, 50 *penniä* and 1 *markka* and four notes, 5, 10, 50 and 100 *markkaa*. This currency, which was introduced in January 1963, replaced an earlier one in which the *markka* was the same value as the present *penni*, thus the *markka* of today is equivalent to 100 of the old *markkaa*. This change in the currency explains why many Finns, when asked the price of some very expensive item will give it in 'old millions' rather than present day rates. Following the devaluations (British and Finnish) of 1967 the official exchange rate was fixed at £1 = 10·05 Fmks, which meant that the 10 *markkaa* note was worth roughly the same as the British £1 note, while $1 equalled 4·20 Fmks. As a result of the monetary adjustments of December 1971 the value of the *markka* was again changed and on 5 June 1973 the exchange rates were: £1 = 9·64 Fmks, $1 = 3·70 Fmks.

In addition to state tax (*valtionvero*), all Finnish residents pay a commune tax (*kunnallisvero*) to the commune in which they live, and like the state tax this one is also an income tax. There are no rates, as in Britain, though of course owners have to pay tax on houses, flats or other real estate. Members of the Lutheran and Orthodox congregations also pay a church tax, equal to about 1 per cent of their income. State and communal taxation is progressive, graduated according to the situation of the individual concerned. There are three basic tax classes: Class I, unmarried persons over twenty-four with no dependents; Class II, single or divorced persons with dependents, and married couples having no children after three years of marriage; Class III, all others. As the lowest rates are found in Class III it is obviously financially advantageous for a single person approaching the age of twenty-four to look round for a marriage partner, though the tax laws might then encourage speedy divorce, as married couples are assessed together for tax purposes except in the year that they marry. According to figures provided by the Central Association of Tax Payers in 1971, a person earning a salary of 20,000 Fmks a year (£1,990, $4,762) would pay 22·5 per cent of his salary in state tax if he was in Class I, 19 cent if in Class II and 16·1 per cent if in Class III. When communal taxation, social security payments and church tax are added, the figures become 40·5 per cent, 37 per cent and 34·1 per cent respectively.

There is little embarrassment in discussing salaries and rates of taxation in Finland, as in many communes an unofficial but highly popular *verokalenteri* (tax calendar) is published each year, which lists the salaries of all members of the commune earning 10,000 Fmks (£995, $2,381) or more. There is no point in being shy about your income if everybody can go and look it up.

Indirect taxes are frequently high, and it is a standing joke that if one buys a car in Finland one buys another for the government. It was estimated in March 1971 that on a car costing £1,556 ($3,734) the purchaser paid £706 ($1,694) in tax.

Businesses as well as individuals pay local and church taxes, though recently schemes have been introduced to give tax benefits to companies with a large export business or to those willing to set up plants in backward parts of the country. Concerns establishing factories in such areas, mainly in the north and east, are granted exemption from certain local and state taxation, for a period of ten years.

In the 1973 budget, state funds were allocated as follows:

Education and culture	17·3%
Social security	10·9%
Health	8·4%
Housing and community schemes	7·1%
Communications	12·7%
Agriculture and forestry	10·9%
Industry	4·5%
Government services	5·4%
Police, security, etc	3·5%
Defence	6·0%
Other expenditure	13·3%

THE ARMED FORCES

The Finnish defence forces are limited in size by the terms of the Treaty of Paris. The army is restricted to 34,400 men, the air force to 3,000 and the navy to 4,500. In addition the armed forces are not permitted to possess guided missiles other than defensive missiles, aircraft primarily designed as bombers, submarines or any kinds of nuclear weapon. The air force is limited to sixty combat machines and the navy to a tonnage of 10,000.

All Finnish males are subject to conscription and are usually called up at twenty, though volunteers are permitted to join the services at the age of seventeen. The Finnish forces in fact consist almost completely of conscripts, with regular officers and a cadre of NCOs and specialists. Military service usually lasts for a period of 240 days, which makes the Finnish conscription period one of the shortest in the world. Men who are selected for the Reserve Officers' School, NCOs and certain specialists serve for 330 days. Those who have ethical or religious objections to bearing arms can either do 'unarmed' service for the defence department, or work in a hospital or similar institution; but only 0·5 per cent of those liable for conscription opt for these alternatives. The majority of the population seems to be in favour of conscription, which means that there is strong social pressure on young men to fulfil their military obligation, not only from the older generation, but also from their peers.

Nevertheless in recent years attitudes seem to have changed somewhat, especially among those taking higher education. Many object to the way military service interferes with their studies, while to an increasing number the whole idea of military service appears irrelevant in modern society.

After completing his military service the conscript is transferred to the reserve where he has certain training obligations, in addition to being liable for call-up in a national emergency.

The commander-in-chief of the defence forces is the President of the Republic, though in wartime he can delegate his authority to a serving officer. The professional head of the forces is usually a general or lieutenant-general, to whom the commanders of the various arms are responsible. Control of the armed forces is vested in the Ministry of Defence (*puolustusministeriö*).

The Finnish army (*armeija*) has a strength of about 32,000 men and can draw on reserves of some 630,000. The country is divided into seven military commands (*sotilasläänit*), each one being allocated a proportion of the ground defence forces. In 1971 the army included 1 armoured brigade, 6 infantry brigades, 8 independent infantry battalions, 2 coastal artillery regiments, 3 coastal artillery battalions and 5 anti-aircraft units, though as in most armies requirements and organisation are constantly changing, while certain units may well be below strength. It is the policy of the Finnish forces to buy military equipment from both East and West, and the armoured brigade is equipped with Russian T-54, T-55 and PT-76 tanks, and also with British-built Charioteers. Anti-tank weapons include the British Vigilant and the French SS-11. Many of the army's requirements, particularly small arms and transport vehicles, are made by domestic industry.

The navy (*merivoimat*) has a strength of 2,500 men, with a further 25,000 or so in reserve. There are two naval bases, one near Helsinki, the other at Turku, and a naval academy at Suomenlinna, the ancient fortress guarding the sea approaches to the capital. The navy is primarily a small-boat force, trained to work in conjunction with the coastal artillery in the defence of the intricate waters of the Gulfs of Finland and Bothnia. The largest unit of the Finnish navy is the training ship *Matti Kurki* (ex-HMS *Porlock Bay*), purchased from Britain in 1962. In 1964 two Riga-class frigates were obtained from the Soviet Union, while in the late sixties two fast corvettes of Finnish design were launched. The smaller units are organised into a patrol flotilla, a gunboat flotilla and a mine flotilla, while there are also a number of other craft, including a missile-armed patrol boat.

The air force (*ilmavoimat*), like the other forces, gets its equipment from a number of sources. Thus during the 1960s the front-line aircraft of the three fighter squadrons of the Finnish air force were Folland Gnats and Mig 21Fs, though the former are due to be replaced by Swedish Drakens. The basic training aircraft of the air force is the Saab Safir, while more advanced training is carried out on Fouga Magisters, many of which were built under licence in Finland. Other training machines include Mig 15s and Mig 21UTIs. The transport squadron is equipped with C-47 and Beaver planes and a number of helicopters. The active strength of the air force is about 3,000 men, with reserves around 30,000.

While it is acknowledged that the Finnish defence forces would be unable to repel a determined attack by a major power, the armed forces are considered to have an important role to play in ensuring that Finland is able to defend her neutrality, and not be 'used' by either East or West in an extended conflict involving northern Europe. As the treaty of 1948 shows, the Soviet Union tends to be suspicious of Finland's relations with the West—in both 1918 and 1941–4 German troops fought alongside Finns against Russian interests—and the Finns feel that they must convince the Soviet Union of their reliability. Many Finns are also worried about the manner in which the Soviet Union will interpret the 1948 treaty in the event of a European crisis. Following the invasion of Czechoslovakia in 1968 a large number of Finns thought that it would be their turn next, and their fears were hardly calmed when the Finnish president disappeared to hold talks with Soviet leaders cruising in a destroyer off the coast of Finland.

In order to guard against surprise attack Finland has an extensive radar system to give advance warning of potential aggression, and it is considered that the available forces are sufficient to protect the country's territorial integrity long enough to enable political initiatives to be taken, or to mobilise reserves. Should a drawn-out conflict ensue it is planned that defence would continue along 'guerilla' lines, while dispersal of the air force would be facilitated by the presence of the reserve landing strips that have been constructed along straight stretches of road in various parts of the country.

The Frontier Guard (*Rajavartiolaitos*), consisting of a land force and a coastguard (*merivartio*), of about 3,000 men, is administered by the Ministry of Internal Affairs, though officers and NCOs are trained by the armed forces.

Not long after Finland joined the United Nations, she was invited to send troops to Sinai as part of the UN peace-keeping force. Since that time Finnish soldiers have served in the Lebanon, Kashmir, Cyprus and Suez under UN auspices. In addition to two officers attached to UN Headquarters in New York, the Finns co-operate with other Nordic countries to provide a stand-by force, the members of which are prepared to participate in peace-keeping operations at short notice.

RELIGION

On paper the Finns might appear to be one of the most religious nations on earth, as about 95 per cent of the population belong to one or other of the churches. The largest of these is the Evangelical Lutheran Church, with a membership of about 4·2 million, about 93 per cent of the inhabitants of Finland. The Orthodox Church of Finland comes next with some 60,000 members, about 1·4 per cent of the population. There are five Roman Catholic parishes in Finland to serve the needs of 2,800 members, the Jehovah's Witnesses have 10,000 members and the Finnish Free Church 8,000. Finland has a Jewish community of about 1,300, and about 900 Muslims.

Both Lutheran and Orthodox Churches are state churches and each parish is entitled to levy a tax on individual church members and companies within its area. Individuals are also encouraged to play an active part in their parish by voting in church elections and attending services. But although the great majority of Finns seem to be content to pay church tax, only a small number are active church members. During 1968 only about 2·6 per cent of the members of the Lutheran Church participated in Sunday services, though the attendance rate for country parishes, 3·3 per cent, was slightly better than that for the urban areas, 1·8 per cent. Most of those who pay church tax probably continue to do so more through habit than conviction, though a powerful inducement for young people, especially girls, is that one cannot get married in church unless one has paid one's church tax as a church member. The 5 per cent or so of the population who belong to no recognised church are entered on a civil register.

The Lutheran Church divides the country into eight dioceses, one of which, Borgå (Porvoo), is administered in Swedish. The oldest diocese, that of Turku, is headed by the Archbishop of the Lutheran Church, who is the Primate of Finland. The dioceses are divided into 72 deaneries, which in turn are divided into 596 parishes. Each of the parishes has a considerable degree of independence, including the right to elect its own clergy.

As we have seen, the Church had considerable power in the Middle Ages and its successor carried on the tradition and still speaks with authority today, particularly in the fields of education and public morality. Priests sit on educational boards and teach religious instruction and religious history in many schools. The comparative wealth of the Church has enabled it to build new churches when necessary, and as a result the country has a number of striking church buildings, including Aalto's *Lakeuden Risti* (Cross of the Plain) church in Seinäjoki, *Kalevan Kirkko* (Kaleva Church) designed by Reima Pietilä and Raili Paatelainen in Tampere, and the recently completed *Temppeliaukion*

Kirkko in Helsinki, which is carved out of the rock. Many of these churches have extensive facilities for parish activities, including meeting rooms, kitchens and in some cases even a sauna.

The Orthodox Church owes allegiance to the Oecumenical Patriarch of Constantinople, and in Finland is divided into the dioceses of Karelia and Helsinki, the former headed by the Archbishop, who has his cathedral in Kuopio.

3

How They Live

HOUSING

At the beginning of the present century 87·5 per cent of the population of Finland lived in country areas, and in 1935 the figure was still between 75 and 80 per cent. Since World War II, however, the Finns have been moving from the country in in-increasing numbers, and in 1971 the urban population exceeded 50 per cent for the first time. In 1935 only four Finnish towns, Helsinki, Viipuri, Turku and Tampere, had more than 30,000 inhabitants; at the beginning of 1972 there were seventeen such communities. This rapid growth of urban centres has produced grave housing problems, which have been accentuated by losses sustained in the war years, when an estimated 120,000 dwellings were either destroyed or ceded to the Soviet Union. Making good these losses took about five years, so that it was not until the 1950s that Finland's housing stock began to exceed the 1939 level. So it is not surprising that in 1960 Finland had one of Europe's worst overcrowding problems, with an average of 1·31 persons to every room. Although by the end of the sixties this figure had improved to 1·11 persons per room, some 50 per cent of the population still lived in two or fewer rooms (a room in this context has a minimum area of 75·3 square feet).

The typical Finnish house of the early 1900s was built of wood, and in the country it might well have been erected by the householder himself, with the help of his neighbours. This custom of communal assistance, *talkoot* (still to be found in some places), was particularly well developed in rural areas, where sometimes the whole community would lend a hand if some major construction work was being undertaken. The household benefiting from the aid was expected to provide the workers with food and drink and, when the job was completed, sauna. In recent years many of the wooden buildings have been demolished, to be replaced by purpose-built flats erected by the most modern construction techniques. At its best Finnish housing is extremely good, but in many country areas and in some of the large towns there are still many inferior dwellings, where families live in cramped conditions with inadequate amenities.

According to the 1960 census the average floor area of a Finnish dwelling was 550 square feet, though the average area of those built during the sixties has been 696 square feet. Compared with their British or American counterparts Finnish homes are rather small, usually consisting of two or three rooms and a kitchen. The average British dwelling built in recent years has had a floor area of about 920 square feet, spread over a kitchen and four or five other rooms. In the United States some 89 per cent of all dwellings have four or more rooms, while 41 per cent have six or more. About 60 per cent of the Finnish housing stock has been built since the war, compared with 38 per cent for Britain and 55 per cent or so for the United States. In 1970 7·9 dwellings per 1,000 inhabitants were completed, compared with 6·9 per 1,000 in the UK and 7·7 per 1,000 in the USA. During the sixties approximately 68 per cent of the residential buildings completed in Finland were in blocks of flats (*kerrostalot*), 25 per cent were *omakotitalot* ('one-family houses'), while the remaining 7 per cent were of the *rivitalo* (row or terrace house) type.

Over 95 per cent of the dwellings completed in the mid-sixties had sewerage, running hot and cold water, a water-closet and central heating, and over 75 per cent had bathrooms. (In many houses of the *omakotitalo* and *rivitalo* type a sauna and shower often take the place of a bath.) On the debit side, in 1969 only just over 44 per cent of farms in Finland had running water, about 50 per cent had sewerage and a mere 15·5 per cent central heating.

Until the middle of the 1960s one of the most popular forms of investment in Finland was to buy a flat and let it. In 1966, however, the tax law was amended in such a way that the return on rented property was reduced, and this, coupled with the stringent rent freeze introduced after the 1967 devaluation, has meant that the number of flats available for rent has declined. It is estimated that there are about 1·4 million homes in Finland, about 60 per cent of which are owner-occupied, the remainder being rented. In Britain about half the 19 million dwellings are owner-occupied, while in the United States there are approximately 53 million dwellings, some 62 per cent of which are occupied by their owners.

It is rare for a flat to be let furnished, but even in an unfurnished flat a cooker, refrigerator and fitted cupboards are virtually always standard equipment, installed when the building is erected. Double-glazing is practically universal and most modern flats will have ample (standardised) electric points, television and radio aerials and a bathroom with a drain in the floor and a shower attachment on the bath. In addition the owner or tenant is given storage space in the attic of the block of flats, and sometimes a cold cellar, too. Most blocks have a sauna, which can be booked for an hour or so each week, while many also have a washing room, with an automatic machine and other facilities. Perhaps the most important man in any block of flats is the *talonmies* (literally: 'houseman') who with his wife keeps the house and its environs clean, takes care of the heating system and clears away the snow during the winter.

When one takes into account the climate in Finland and the resultant heating, snow-clearing and maintenance problems, the advantages of living in a flat are fairly obvious. The drawbacks are similar to those which accompany flat-dwelling everywhere: thin walls and noisy neighbours, lack of privacy, cramped living conditions and lack of easy access. This last disadvantage is aggravated in Finland by the fact that the street-door is almost invariably locked at eight or nine in the evening. As few blocks have outside door-bells, residents are completely isolated from the outside world unless they possess a telephone.

This can, of course, have its advantages, but if one is entertaining one's guests must be well trained, otherwise one will spend the greater part of the evening downstairs opening the street-door.

Although in many ways flats are very convenient in Finnish conditions there seems little doubt that given the choice—and the money—most Finns would opt for a house of their own. Many blocks of flats in Finland are built by housing companies which then sell to individuals shares equal to the value of one dwelling unit; the buyers thus become the owners of a flat. In an attempt to relieve the overcrowding problem, during the sixties the state stepped up rates of assistance to those who wished to purchase dwellings for their own use. In 1961 36 per cent of the 37,300 residences completed were subsidised by the state. In 1970 49,740 dwellings were built, 44 per cent of which received state assistance. In 1972 the state housing grant was £71 million ($186 million) for 28,500 dwellings. State loans are channelled through the Housing Production Committee—ARAVA—which was established in 1949. In 1970 19·1 per cent of the finance for housing came from the commercial banks, 22·3 per cent from the savings and co-operative banks, 17·6 per cent from the state, while 23·4 per cent came from individuals. Insurance companies, the Post Office Bank and a number of other concerns contributed the balance. It is estimated that about 40·2 per cent of the dwellings were built for private persons, 40·1 per cent for housing companies, and the bulk of the remainder for the state, communes or industrial concerns. Those whose income is too low to buy a home can apply for government help with their rent or with the acquisition of a dwelling in a government-subsidised housing co-operative. Housing subsidies are also provided for old-age pensioners in need.

During the sixties the average contribution of the building and construction industry to the Finnish gross national product was 9·4 per cent. The industry employs about 10 per cent of the economically active population, that is about 122,000 workers. In order to speed up construction and thus save money on wages and delays caused by the climate, extensive prefabrication is employed in the Finnish construction industry. Staircases, bathroom units and wall sections are all made in the factory, ready to be swung into place on the site. The National Housing Board takes an active interest in developing new techniques, using traditional building materials such as wood and concrete, and also newer ones like fibreglass and plastics.

SAUNA

Although the average foreigner might view an invitation to spend the evening in a bath with mixed feelings, the sauna (pronounced 'sow- [the pig] -na') is an extremely enjoyable experience, particularly if the surroundings and company are good (mixed sauna it should be mentioned is not the rule). The pleasantest saunas are those attached to summer cottages, by the side of a lake or the sea, so that participants can go straight into the water from the hot room, the temperature of which is usually between 176 and 230° F.

ARCHITECTURE AND DESIGN

It is particularly appropriate to mention Finnish architecture and design under the heading 'How They Live', for in recent years good design and planning have become an essential part of the Finnish way of life. The essence of modern design in Finland is that virtually any article in general use can and should be attractive as well as functional, and that in fact the two are complementary. This simple, but all too frequently ignored concept has been applied with great success to a wide range of articles, including pottery, glassware, cutlery, textiles, furniture and housing.

It is still possible to see the first successful example of Finnish town planning carried out by Engels and Ehrenström around the Senate Square—*Senaatintori*—in Helsinki, during the first half of the nineteenth century. There are also a number of buildings surviving from the age of the National Romantic Movement, including Tampere Cathedral, the work of Lars Sonck and the National Museum in Helsinki, designed by Lindgren and Saarinen. Eliel Saarinen's best-known work is undoubtedly the railway station in Helsinki, hated, admired, but impossible to ignore. In 1922 Saarinen moved to the United States and continued his career in that country, having a considerable influence on the development of American architecture. Alvar Aalto and Viljo Rewell are also architects whose work is well known in the New World as well as Europe, one of Rewell's most famous buildings being Toronto City Hall.

The migration to the towns which has occurred since the war has meant that outside many urban centres suburbs have developed, giving exciting opportunities to architects and town-planners. The most famous of these new suburbs is the 'garden city' of Tapiola, outside Helsinki, which was first established in 1951. Other commissions for architects have come from the Church, industrial concerns, banks and other businesses, while the state and municipal authorities have also made a contribution.

SERVANTS

The number of living-in servants has decreased greatly in recent years, though well-off professional households, particularly those where both husband and wife are working, may still employ a housekeeper or maid. The relatively small size of the average Finnish flat tends to render the charlady superfluous, but in some cases one is employed for heavy cleaning, earning about 50p ($1.23) an hour.

Just as in Britain and the United States, some families, particularly those with small children, may employ au pair girls, usually from Britain or Germany. But whereas au pairs go to Britain or the United States to study English, Finns employing British or German girls do so to improve their children's (or their own) language skills. Mothers who wish to get small children off their hands for a couple of hours during the day can entrust them to a *puisto-täti* (park-aunt), who will keep an eye on them while mother is shopping or doing the housework. Day nurseries are rare and all have a long waiting list; it was estimated in 1972 that only 9 per cent of children needing day-nursery places in fact get them.

The Finns tend to be unimaginative about food, and the emphasis is usually on quantity rather than on quality or variety. Apart from the ubiquitous potato, the Finn eats few vegetables; the annual consumption is estimated to be only about 36lb per head. Before the advent of frozen foods the amount must have been even less, as fresh vegetables—even if available—tend to be very expensive during the winter.

The most popular meat is beef, per capita consumption in 1970 being about 42lb, followed by pork, per capita consumption in 1970 being 40lb. A large variety of sausages are available: the *nakkimakkara* is a close cousin of the frankfurter, while *berliinimakkara* and *teemakkara* also have a German ancestry. There are, however, a number of Finnish specialities, including *poromakkara* (reindeer sausage) and *saunamakkara*, which is placed on top of the sauna stove or grilled over an open fire after sauna. Meat balls (*lihapullat*), the Finnish fish and chips, are as popular in Finland as they are in Sweden, while the Finns also share the Swedish enthusiasm for the open sandwich (*voileipä*) and the standard of these is usually quite good. Some Finnish delicacies should be approached with care, including *kaalikääryle* (minced meat wrapped in cabbage), while the famous Savo delicacy *kalakukko* (Finland's answer to the Cornish pasty, consisting of fish and fat pork baked in pastry) is not to everybody's taste. *Karjalanpaisti* (a stew made from pork, veal and mutton) is a truly delicious dish, though unfortunately not on the menu of many eating-houses.

Soups of all kinds make up an important part of the Finnish

diet and often form the main dish at a meal, particularly in the case of *hernekeitto* (pea soup), traditionally eaten on Thursdays. Other soups include *kesäkeitto* (a vegetable soup), *lihakeitto* (meat soup) and *kalakeitto* (fish soup). Fish, however, is not confined to the soup bowl, and large amounts of fresh and salt-water fish are eaten throughout the year, salted and smoked *silakka* (Baltic herring) being regarded as a particular delicacy. Salmon and trout are found in many Finnish rivers and on many dining tables too, but the fish that has a season to itself is the *rapu* (crayfish), which provides the basic—though expensive —dish at a large number of parties in late July and August. One of the traditional Christmas dishes is boiled *lipeäkala* (cod), which is followed by *riisipuro*, a dish which resembles un-sweetened rice-pudding. Fortunately this somewhat spartan fare is supplemented by *joulukinkku* (Christmas ham) which, like most Finnish pork and ham, is of high quality. Bread is still made at home in many country areas, but in towns a large range of bread can be obtained from the *leipomo* or bakery.

Excess drinking is a major social problem in Finland, but it appears from the figures that the liquid Finns are most addicted to is milk rather than alcohol. In 1971 the Finns consumed just over 482 pints of milk products a head, mainly in the form of milk and cream and various types of sour milk, such as *piimä*, *kefiiri*, *viili* and yoghurt. Finns are rather suspicious about making tea and prefer to leave the actual process in the hands of the tea-drinker, providing a cup of boiling water and a tea-bag, thus evading responsibility for the finished product. They are very fond of coffee, however—nine times as much coffee is drunk in Finland as in Britain—and coffee-making is an art they have studied with great care, with the result that Finnish coffee is usually delicious.

The sale and production of alcohol is controlled by the state monopoly, Oy Alko Ab. From 1919 to 1932 there was prohibition in Finland, but as in many other countries the prohibition experiment failed and had the undesired effect of producing a massive crime wave. A British newspaper writing when prohibition was at its height commented: 'of the 168,217 arrests [in

E

Finland] in the past year . . . 123,000 are directly attributed to Prohibition. The remaining 45,000 [are] mainly assault cases, arising out of drunken fights.' Following public pressure, prohibition was repealed in 1932, though the sale of alcohol has remained a state monopoly since that time.

Today the *juoppo* is very much part of the Finnish scene, and it is by no means unusual to see drunks wandering around the streets, often in groups of two or three. In many cases a team may be doing a round of the rubbish bins in the hope that they can find something worth selling, while others just stagger about aimlessly. The presence of this 'drop-out' population is one of the reasons why street-doors are locked so early, an action which is perhaps symbolic, as the majority of Finns seem indifferent to the fate of the alcoholic. There are, however, a number of institutions, including an Alcoholics Anonymous group, which try to provide assistance, and a certain proportion of the profits from Alko go to finance research into the problems of alcoholism.

Alko produces, imports, exports and sells alcoholic beverages, and also grants licences to breweries and restaurants. It runs 167 shops, and in 1970 granted licences for the sale of alcohol on the premises to 1,182 establishments. Until January 1970 the only place where one could buy alcohol for home consumption was an Alko shop, but since that date *keskiolut* (middle or Class III) beer has been on sale in grocery shops—at the end of 1970 16,736 shops had licences for the sale of *keskiolut*. Stronger beer, wines and spirits can still only be obtained from the official Alko shops, and every week on Friday evenings and Saturday mornings one can see large numbers of men with brief-cases and preoccupied expressions bearing down on these shops from all sides, while the sign of an impending holiday is queues which sometimes stretch out into the street. Much of the alcoholic liquor on sale in Alko shops is imported, but Finland produces a number of different kinds of spirits, including *Koskenkorva*—the basis of many a Finnish cocktail and drunken evening—and liqueurs such as *Mesimarja* and *Lakka*.

For many Finns breakfast (*aamiainen*) tends to be a snatched meal taken early in the day, as the working day starts at eight. Frequently a cup of coffee and a piece of *pulla* (a sweet bread-like bun) or one of the variety of 'hard breads', of which Finns are very fond, is made to suffice. Largely because of the frugality of the first meal, lunch (*lounas*) is usually taken at about eleven or twelve, and consists of a meat dish or soup with a sandwich. Children are provided with lunch at school, and each week the menu is published in the local paper so that parents can see what their offspring are eating. *Päivällinen* or dinner is served between five and six—later if one is entertaining—and is a meat or fish dish followed by a sweet and accompanied by the inevitable glass of milk.

Restaurants (*ravintolat*) tend to be rather expensive; a straightforward three-course meal could easily cost £6–£7 ($15.72–$18.34) for two. Eating out in Finland can rarely be described as a memorable gastronomic experience, though the food is usually well prepared and served in pleasant surroundings. Unfortunately many restaurants seem to be of the opinion that food should appeal to the eye rather than the palate, which means that only too often the food is attractively displayed and garnished, but rapidly cooling by the time it arrives on the diner's plate, which is itself almost invariably cold. Probably the best value in a Finnish restaurant is the *voileipäpöytä*, the Finnish version of *smörgåsbord*, which many places provide at lunchtime. The basic price is about £1 ($2.45) and for this one can visit the 'cold', 'hot' and 'sweet' tables as often as one wishes.

Service in restaurants is often slow, but nevertheless a service charge of 13 per cent is always added to the bill. Every restaurant door is guarded by a large *vahtimestari* or porter, whose job is to scrutinise all would-be customers. Although admittance policy has been liberalised considerably in recent years, men without ties and women with trousers are still anathema to some *vahtimestarit*. On leaving a restaurant one is expected to tip the *vahtimestari* about fifty pennies or a mark, partly for assisting with one's coat and partly, one sometimes feels, in gratitude for being allowed in in the first place.

Compared with similar institutions in Britain the standard of food and drink provided by most Finnish cafés of the *baari* or *kahvila* type is quite high (the coffee served in Finnish railway-station snack bars, for example, puts the brew served by British Rail to shame). But Finland can offer nothing resembling the British pub. A number of *grillibaarit*, midway in standard and price between the *baari* and *ravintola* proper have taken advantage of the recent change in attitude towards drinking, and have tried to model themselves on the English public house. One of these, run by students in Turku, even went so far as putting pictures of the British royal family on the wall in an attempt to create the appropriate atmosphere.

HOW THEY SPEND THEIR MONEY

The internationally famous double-act 'Prices and Incomes' has also had a long run on the Finnish economic stage in recent years. For reasons examined in more detail in the next chapter, Finland faced grave economic difficulties following World War II, and it was not until the early 1950s that the pre-war standard of living was surpassed. By the late fifties and early sixties, however, conditions had improved, and between 1960 and 1964 household incomes rose by 57 per cent—faster than in any other West European country. During the same period consumer prices rose by 20 per cent. By 1965 the increase in incomes had slowed down, but consumption was still rising by between 6 and 7 per cent a year. Unfortunately for the balance of payments situation much of this consumption was in the form of imported goods, and in an attempt to improve the trade balance the Finnmark was devalued in October 1967 and a prices and incomes policy was introduced.

Wage increases in Finland are usually linked to the cost of living index. But following the 1967 devaluation, the government, the representatives of the employers and the unions got together and agreed that, in order to obtain the maximum benefit from the measure, increases in prices and incomes should be kept to a minimum, at approximately 3 to 4 per cent per year. It was evident, however, that towards the end of the 1970 the unions were becoming increasingly restive about the agreement. Discussions between unions and employers failed to resolve the situation and matters were at a deadlock when President Kekkonen intervened personally. The result of this intervention, the UKK agreement (so called because of the president's initials) allowed for an average pay rise of between 8 and 9 per cent. Kekkonen estimated that during 1971 the rise in wage-earners' real incomes would be about 5 per cent. This occurred but it was accompanied by inflation, and in March 1972 a new agreement was hammered out, the HL agreement (after the chief negotiators, Hämäläinen and Laatunen). This proposed a new minimum wage of £0.33 ($0.81) an hour, £56 ($137.7) a month. The average pay rise envisaged by the HL agreement was 7·2 per cent.

In 1972 a worker in the metal industry was earning about £0.60 ($1.47) an hour, while the average salary of a secondary school teacher was about £186 ($456.4) a month. A university professor's income was about £411 ($1,007.8) and a hospital doctor's £331 ($811) a month. Between 1964 and 1969 the annual increase in hourly earnings was 9·1 per cent, while over the same period consumer prices rose by 5·3 per cent. In Britain hourly earnings increased 6 per cent and prices 4·3 per cent, in the United States the figures were 4·8 and 3·4 per cent respectively. Today the Finn has more money to spend than ever before and a greater range of goods and services to spend it on.

As Finland has become more industrialised and urbanised since the last war, so patterns of consumer expenditure have changed, to resemble those in other developed countries. In the last decade the average growth rate of the volume of private consumption was 4·7 per cent, the fastest-growing sectors being services, entertainment, transport and durable goods. Food, although still the largest single item of household expenditure, takes a smaller proportion of the family income than earlier, and the same is true of other essential goods. The number of labour-saving appliances and other household durables used in Finnish homes has increased in recent years, and at the end of the sixties 71 per cent of Finnish households had refrigerators (UK: 61%, USA: 99%), 58 per cent washing machines (UK: 66%, USA: 55%), and 33 per cent electric mixers (UK: 23%, USA: 67%), while 204 out of every 1,000 Finns had a telephone (UK: 218/1,000, USA: 523/1,000) and 216 out of every 1,000 a television set (UK: 286/1,000, USA: 409/1,000). The number of private cars in Finland has risen from 183,267 in 1960 to 711,968 in 1970, which means that there is a car for every eight persons; in the United Kingdom there is one for every five and in the United States one for every two. In 1969 private consumption per head in Finland was about £442 ($1,060), compared with £513 ($1,230) in Britain and £1,187 ($2,850) in the USA.

It is estimated that at the end of the last decade the average Finnish family was spending about £22 ($52.8) a week on housekeeping, the expenditure being divided up as follows: food and drink 34% (UK: 30%, USA: 21%); rent 10% (12%, 14%); fuel and light 4% (5%, 4%); furniture and household operation 8% (8%, 11%); clothing 9% (10%, 9%); health and hygiene 4% (2%, 9%); transport 14% (13%, 15%); recreation 7% (8%, 6%); tobacco 3% (6%, 2%); miscellaneous 7% (6%, 9%).

Internal trade in Finland is dominated by four large wholesale groups, two of which, Suomen Tukkukauppiaiden Lütto (STL) with over 330 members and Kesko Oy, which has nearly 15,000 shareholders, are private. SOK and OTK are co-operatives; the former has about 280 member societies with 4,440 retail outlets, the latter 81 member societies and about 3,730 shops. Between them these four groups dominate the food trade and also play an important part in the supply of other goods.

The whole pattern of retail trade in Finland has changed considerably in recent years. In 1962 there were only 870 self-service shops and supermarkets in the country; at the end of the sixties there were over 3,400, while the first hypermarkets are being developed on the outskirts of some of the larger towns. It is estimated that about 16 per cent of Finnish foodshops are self-service (in the USA the figure is 95 per cent), and between 67 and 70 per cent of these are in private hands (35 per cent of them belonging to the K-marketing system supplied by Kesko) while the remainder are owned by co-operative societies. In spite of the trend towards supermarkets there are still a large number of 'corner shops' in Finnish towns, many of them occupying purpose-built premises in new blocks of flats.

Probably the best-known department store in Finland is Stockmann's, its massive frontage dominating Mannerheimin-tie, Helsinki's principal thoroughfare, and with branches in Tampere and Pietarsaari. Both SOK and OTK have developed chains of stores, the former having over 110 branches, the latter about half as many. In 1970 the total value of retail trade in Finland was about £1,554 million ($3,721 million).

SOCIAL SECURITY

While the Finnish system of social security is not as developed as that of the United Kingdom, it is considerably more so than in the United States. The aim of the Finnish system is to ensure that sickness, old age or unemployment should not place too great a burden on the individual or his or her family. In 1970 social security expenditure amounted to £583.7 million ($1,400.9 million), 32 per cent of which was paid by the state, 20 per cent by the local authorities, 39 per cent by the employers and the remaining 9 per cent by the general public. Old-age and disability pensions accounted for 42·8 per cent of total expenditure, health for 27·5 per cent, family welfare for 11·9 per cent, while the remainder went on public assistance, accident insurance and payments to war casualties.

Medical services

Statutory sickness insurance came into force in July 1961, though before that date subsidised treatment had been available in hospitals run by communes and extensive voluntary sickness insurance existed. The Sickness Insurance Act does not provide free medical treatment, but anyone who has to visit a doctor can apply to the sickness insurance office for a refund of 60 per cent of the doctor's fee. A refund of 75 per cent is given for any treatment or examination exceeding £0.56 ($1.37). If medicines costing more than £0.37 ($0.90) are required as part of the treatment, 50 per cent of their price can be recovered, while medicines for the treatment of chronic or serious illnesses are repaid in full. Patients can also recover the cost of transport to and from hospital or doctor if the fare is more than £0.23 ($.56). Hospital fees are not refunded because patients are only charged 10 per cent of the cost of treatment, the remainder being borne by communal or state funds.

Every insured person who is unable to work due to sickness is entitled to a daily allowance (*päiväraha*), the amount paid usually being about 45 per cent of the recipient's salary. The lowest rate of *päiväraha* (mid-1972) is £0.70 ($1.71) and the highest, for someone whose income exceeds 25,500 mk (£2,372, $5,811) a year, is £3.56 ($8.73). Supplements are also paid to support the recipient's family when necessary. Payment of *päiväraha* begins seven days after the onset of the illness.

The maternity allowance (*äitiysraha*) is calculated on the same basis as *päiväraha*, the minimum grant being £50.23 ($123) for a woman who is not working. A working mother gets up to 45 per cent of her salary during the seventy-two days' maternity leave (*äitiysloma*) to which every expectant mother is entitled. In addition to the maternity grant each mother is given an *äitiysavustuspakkaus*, which contains a variety of clothing and other necessities for the new baby (and, as a gesture to the family-planning lobby, a packet of contraceptives). Over

50,000 of these boxes are distributed each year. Child allowances are paid for all children, the rates being: £21.21 ($51.96) a year for the first child, £25.30 ($59.72) for the second and £30.14 ($73.84) for subsequent children.

Dental care is not covered by sickness insurance, and although proposals have been made that expectant mothers and children under seventeen should receive free dental treatment, these have not been implemented yet. However, at the beginning of 1972 the government published a five-year health plan which included free dental care for children born since 1960. The plan also gave details of an ambitious scheme to introduce a medical service for the country as a whole, the most important element of which is to be the health centre (*terveyskeskus*). Each health centre will be staffed by a team of doctors, dentists and nurses, and serve a community of about 10,000 people. But there is a danger that the scheme may run into difficulties outside urban centres, as many doctors consider that the inducements to live in rural areas are insufficient. It is estimated that the introduction of the new scheme will cost at least £26 million ($63 million) during 1973, £4.6 million ($11.2 million) of which will go on the building of health centres. Another large item will be salaries, for it is estimated that 70 additional doctors and 100 extra dentists will be required, together with 30 nurses and about 800 other members of staff.

There are about 330 hospitals in Finland, with approximately 50,000 beds altogether. There are about 4,200 doctors, which gives a ratio of 0·88 doctors to every 1,000 patients, compared with 1·15:1,000 in Britain and 1·58:1,000 in the United States. Dentists number 2,500, while there are over 22,000 nurses. Maternity classes and pre-natal care are given in the 2,000 or so maternity clinics (*äitiysneuvolat*). There are also about 3,200 child welfare clinics (*lastenneuvolat*) which provide care from birth to school-age, ie seven.

In order to qualify as a doctor (*lääkäri*) a student must attend one of the five medical schools in the country, in Helsinki, Tampere, Turku, Oulu or Kuopio. Dentists (*hammaslääkärit*) are trained in Turku, Oulu and Helsinki. Both dentists and doctors enjoy high social status and good salaries, which probably explains why the competition for entry to medical schools is extremely keen. A large proportion of both dentists and doctors are women.

Pensions

Finland's first Old Age Pensions Act was passed in 1937, but the coming of the war made it impossible to put it into effect, and so supplementary measures were applied until the National Pensions Act of 1957. Under this act all Finnish residents aged 65 and over are entitled to receive a pension. At the beginning of 1972 the basic pension rate was £7.16 ($18.76) a month, £85.95 ($225.12) a year, and this sum is tied to the cost of living index. In addition to the basic pension there are schemes for pensions based on earnings. The first of these came into operation in July 1962 when the *työntekijäin eläkelaki* (TEL)— the Workers' Pension Act—and the *lyhytaikaisissa työsuhteissa olevien työntekijäin eläkelaki* (LEL)—the Short-term Workers' Pension Act—were introduced. The first act applied to permanent workers, the second to temporary or seasonal workers. The basic concept behind these schemes is to provide a pension related to earnings, the actual amount depending on the worker's length of service, last salary and date of birth. The size of the pension is calculated by multiplying 1 per cent of the worker's final pay by his length of service in years. The maximum permitted pension is 42 per cent of the final salary. In the case of LEL the pension is calculated from the worker's mean annual earnings from manual labour. By the terms of TEL every employer must arrange a pension for his workers, and this is usually done by making an arrangement with an insurance company or by setting up a pension fund. Each job lasting more than four months carries full pension rights, and thus a change of employment does not mean that one loses the right to a pension.

In 1970 two further schemes were introduced, *yrittäjien*

eläkelaki (YEL) applying to self-employed persons, and *maata-lousyrittäjien eläkelaki* (MYEL) for farmers. Like the TEL and LEL schemes these are compulsory, and mean that the state ensures that self-employed persons put away a certain proportion of their income for their old age. The maximum pension under YEL and MYEL is also 42 per cent of the income on which it is based. There are separate pension acts for state and local government employees and those in the service of the state churches. Soldiers who saw active service during the wars are entitled to a pension, the rate of which varies according to the recipient's circumstances. Supplementary payments are available to pensioners in cases of hardship, and to cover things like housing and medical care.

The body which co-ordinates the various pension schemes is *Eläketurvakeskus* (The Central Pension Security Institute) which maintains a register of all insured persons. In 1970 £130.9 million ($314.2 million) was paid out in pensions, £358,209 ($859,702) a day.

Unemployment funds

There are a number of unemployment funds, financed partly by the state, partly by a central unemployment fund, which receives money from employers, and partly from membership fees. In 1970 there were seventy-seven of these funds and they paid out benefits totalling £8.7 million ($20.9 million) to 86,241 of their 796,383 members.

4

How They Work

As we have already seen, at the beginning of the twentieth century the great majority of Finns lived in rural areas and most of them depended on agriculture for a living. Although the situation had changed somewhat from 1850, when 90 per cent of the population were employed in agriculture, at independence in 1917 66 per cent of the working population still worked on farms or in forestry. The years between the achievement of independence and the outbreak of the Winter War saw a considerable expansion in Finland's industrial capacity, but in 1938 the manufacturing industries were producing only 26 per cent of the net national product, and employed 19 per cent of the labour force. The figures for the agricultural and forestry sector were 35 per cent and 51 per cent respectively.

The wars between 1939 and 1944 were extremely costly to Finland, as in addition to the great loss of life and the expense of munitions she was forced to cede 10 per cent of her land area to the victorious Soviet Union. This land included the important commercial centre of Viipuri, an immense amount of productive capacity, and property estimated to be worth £112.5 million ($450 million) at 1944 prices. In addition the Russians imposed reparations amounting to £75 million ($300 million) on the Finns, to be paid in the form of ships, machinery, pulp and paper, and wood. Manufactured goods made up 60 per cent of the total and this seemed to present an impossible task for a nation whose pre-war industrial capacity had been little more than adequate for her own needs. The price of the goods demanded in reparations was fixed at the 1938 level, which meant that when this factor was added to the cost of establishing the plant necessary to produce the articles required and the purchase of raw material from abroad, the real cost of an item, such as a ship, was many times the price that the Russians paid for it. In 1948 the Russians made modifications to the amounts to be paid, and extended the period over which deliveries had to be made from six to eight years. Even so the cost to the Finnish economy was immense, and it has been estimated that, all told, the cost of the reparations was in the region of £173 million ($700 million).

In spite of the great burden of the reparations, a burden that was psychological as well as physical, they also provided a certain stimulus for Finnish industry. There were many who feared that, after the last consignment of goods had disappeared over the Russian frontier in September 1952, the shipyards and other industrial plant established to meet the reparation demands would become redundant. This, however, did not happen; instead industrial capacity expanded. In 1970 manufacturing industries accounted for 31 per cent of the net national product and employed 27 per cent of the labour force, while agriculture and forestry contributed 14 per cent to the net national product and gave work to 21 per cent of the labour force.

Despite the increased prosperity brought about by the expansion of production—Finland's national income rose from £445 million ($1,068 million) in 1950 to £3,310.5 million ($7,945 million) in 1970—there have been grave economic difficulties, and in October 1967 the *markka* was devalued by 31·25 per cent. In order that the full benefit could be obtained from this measure a plan to stabilise prices and incomes was put into effect, as described in the chapter 'How They Live'. In spite of the fact that Britain, one of Finland's leading trade partners, devalued only a month after Finland, the immediate effects of Finland's action were very encouraging. The £62.2 million ($149.2 million) deficit of 1967 was turned into a £10.2 million

($24.5 million) surplus in 1968, while between 1968 and 1969 the average change in the volume of industrial production was 12·9 per cent and between 1969 and 1970 8·8 per cent, compared with 3·4 and 2 per cent for the United Kingdom, and 4·4 and −2·7 for the United States. During 1970, however, there was a slowing down in demand for Finnish goods, both at home and abroad, and this, accompanied by an increase in demand for foreign goods, produced a deficit of £138 million ($331 million) for the year. There were also signs that the prices and incomes policy was about to fall apart, and at the beginning of 1971 the UKK agreement gave a more than 8 per cent increase in earnings, compared with the 3 to 4 per cent established following devaluation. This, however, was not sufficient for workers in the metal and construction industries and they went on strike, thus adding to the difficulties of the economy. Demand continued to fall off, and the monthly trade figures persistently revealed a deficit, so that by the end of the year the trade account was £172 million ($451 million) in the red. Export earnings had risen a mere 2 per cent over 1970, while the volume of exports actually fell. In December 1971, as a result of the change in the value of the dollar, there was an effective devaluation of about 5 per cent. Although the trade figures for 1972 showed an improvement, the deficit was about £100 million ($245 million), anxiety over the economy still remains.

FOREST-BASED INDUSTRY

The name that the Finns give to their forests, *vihreä kulta* (green gold) gives some indication of the importance that wood holds in the national economy. Moreover green gold has a great advantage over the yellow variety in being raw material that constantly renews itself and, given skilful cultivation, actually increases. Until recently timber was being felled at a faster rate than it was being replaced, but as a result of the TEHO and MERA programmes, introduced in the sixties, this trend has been reversed. New areas have been made available for forest

cultivation by draining swamps, while in some places the practice of centuries has been reversed as low-productive farming
land is planted with trees.

With about 70 per cent of the land area of the country
covered with trees, Finland has the third largest forest area in
Europe, after the Soviet Union and Sweden, totalling about
52·5 million acres, just over 11 acres for every inhabitant. It is
estimated that there are about 1,450 million cubic metres of
wood, 43 per cent of which is pine, 35 per cent spruce and 18
per cent birch. The annual cut is in the region of 50 million
cubic metres and according to the MERA III programme this
will increase to 55 million cubic metres in 1975.

In the days when the world's ships were built of wood the
chief value of the Finnish forests lay in the coniferous trees used
for masts and spars and the pitch and tar that were important
by-products. Britain's interest in the Baltic during the days of
sail lay in the fact that much of the material used in her shipyards came from Finland and Sweden. Many of the stockpiles
of timber and tar burnt in Finnish ports by British naval forces
during the Crimean War were destined for Britain, and following the custom of the time much of the material destroyed had
actually been paid for.

Following experiments in the 1860s that showed that it was
possible to make paper from wood in commercial quantities,
mills were established in various parts of Finland. From the
1880s onwards these centres, around which small communities
soon grew up to form the characteristic factory towns like
Jämsänkoski, Mänttä and Valkeakoski, were to play a vital part
in the economic development of the country. At the present
time there are over sixty mills in Finland, producing pulp by
mechanical, chemical or semi-mechanical methods. In 1970 the
total production of pulp was about 6·2 million tons, 1·05
million tons of which was exported. Much of the pulp is further
processed into paper and board, and in 1970 Finland produced
over 3 million tons of paper in her 28 paper mills, 1·3 million
tons of which was newsprint. Finnish paper is exported to a
total of 130 countries, though her best customers are the United

Kingdom and West Germany. Production of paperboard in 1970 was 1·2 million tons, over a million tons of which was exported.

Major companies in the pulp and paper industry (most of which have interests in other fields too) include the state-controlled Enso-Gutzeit Oy, Oy Nokia Ab, Kymin Oy— Kymmene Ab and Yhtyneet Paperitehtaat Oy (United Paper Mills).

There are more than 500 sawmills producing wood for export and a further 11,000 concentrating on domestic production. In 1970 7·3 million cubic metres of sawn timber were produced, 1·7 million cubic metres of which were exported to Britain. Other important customers included the Netherlands and West Germany. Plywood, fibreboard, chipboard and hardboard are also made, often utilising the waste products of the sawmill industry.

In 1960 the forest-based industry accounted for over 68 per cent of Finland's exports, earning £283 million ($680 million). By 1970 the share of the forest industry in exports had declined to 54·6 per cent, but their value had risen to £525 million ($1,260 million). In 1970 the total value of production in the pulp and paper industry was £601 million ($1,442 million) and in the

————

About 20 per cent of the timber used in factories is carried by water

Smoke rising from a sauna in central Finland

wood industry, £402 million ($965 million). The pulp and paper industry employs about 93,000 workers, the wood industry about 74,000.

Products of the Finnish furniture industry, which includes firms such as Asko, Tehokaluste, Sotka and Lepokalusto, have become very popular both in Finland and abroad in recent years. Although originally based on timber, designers in the industry have for some time been using materials such as fibreglass, metal, plastics and fabrics with considerable success. In 1970 the gross value of production in the furniture industry was £53 million ($127 million) and the number of employees was 23,000.

THE METAL AND ENGINEERING INDUSTRIES

Between 1938 and 1970 production in the metal and engineering industries increased more than six times, while the contribution of these industries to exports rose from 4·3 per cent to 25·2 per cent over the same period. The fastest-growing areas have been shipbuilding, machinery and consumer goods. In the last-mentioned area in particular a number of firms have chal-

———

Lake Saimaa

The design of the Suommu hotel in Lapland is based on the old Lapp tent

lenged imported products successfully. Thus, for example, 80 per cent of the television sets sold in the country are home-produced, while about half the tyres used on motor-vehicles registered in Finland come from Finnish factories.

Mining and basic metal production

Finland's wealth tends to lie above rather than below ground level, and much of the raw material for use in industry must be imported. About 400,000 tons of iron ore are mined in Finland each year, and twice as much is imported, together with scrap iron to produce pig iron and steel. In 1970 the iron and steel industry produced 1·1 million tons of pig iron, 1·2 million tons of crude steel and 800,000 tons of rolled steel. During the early seventies the introduction of new plant will considerably increase capacity in this sector. It is hoped that the production of rolled steel will soon exceed a million tons, and that of crude steel 2 million tons. Much of the iron ore used in the country is imported from Sweden, but in 1971 the Soviet Union proposed that Finnish industry should develop the resources of the Kostamus area in Soviet Karelia.

Finland is Europe's leading producer of high quality copper, 34,000 tons in 1970, while nickel, aluminium, zinc and rarer metals such as vanadium and titanium are also important. Recently new deposits of copper and nickel have been found in eastern Finland and the production of these metals is expected to rise to 2·5 million tons in the seventies. In 1970 zinc production amounted to 56,000 tons, 80 per cent of which was exported. In 1970 the gross value of production in the basic metal industries was £253 million ($607 million) and in metal mining £37 million ($89 million). The value of exports was £59 million ($142 million) in the former and £1.7 million ($4.2 million) in the latter. The labour force in the mining industry was about 4,000, and in the basic metal industries 13,000.

Manufacturing and mechanical engineering

One of the most important branches of the manufacturing industry is that which produces equipment for forestry. Items included in this category range from felling and timber-handling machinery for use in forests, through specialised transport equipment to paper-making machines. One of the leading producers of these machines is the state-controlled Valmet concern, which is also responsible for a large range of other manufactured goods, including tractors, ships, mechanical handling equipment and the rolling stock for the new Helsinki 'metro'. In 1969 Valmet and the Swedish Saab company established a car production plant at Uusikaupunki, which is designed to make 15,000 passenger cars a year. Suomen Autoteollisuus (Finnish Motor Industries) produced 1,200 vehicles in 1970, most of them heavy lorries and buses, 200 of which were exported.

Other large companies operating in the metal manufacturing area include Rauma-Repola Oy, which builds ships and also produces paper-making machines, motors and a wide range of other items, and Kone Oy, the largest crane and lift manufacturer in the Nordic countries, which in 1970 exported more than 2,000 lifts. Lokomo Oy, a subsidiary of Rauma-Repola, produces road-making equipment and also provides the Finnish State Railways with many of their engines and much of their rolling stock. There are also a large number of other firms making products ranging from cutlery and washing-machines to heavy machinery and guns.

Shipbuilding

Between 1929 and 1938 the total output of the Finnish shipbuilding industry was a mere 23,000 tons, so when the Russian reparations demanded 365,000 tons of shipping it was obvious that a great deal of expansion was necessary. In 1970 Finnish shipyards completed 46 vessels totalling 257,000 gross registered tons. Although not a large tonnage by international standards —one super-tanker can be larger than the entire Finnish production for a year—Finnish shipyards have built up a considerable reputation for specialist vessels. The most important of these are ice-breakers; over half those in use in the world today are the products of Finnish yards. A considerable number of car-ferries and container ships have also been built for customers at home and abroad. Countries with ships on order in Finnish yards at the beginning of 1972 included such well-known shipbuilding nations as Sweden, West Germany, Norway and Britain. In 1970 ships represented the largest group of exports in the metal manufacturing industry, 25·3 per cent, worth £62 million ($149 million), a 20 per cent increase on 1969. The best customer was the Soviet Union which took half the output.

Electricity and electronics

The Finnish electrical industry produces a wide range of items including electric motors, power station generators, cable equipment and a large number of electrical appliances. Although the largest and best-known companies are probably Rosenlew and Strömberg, there are a number of smaller concerns such as Vaisala, whose metrological equipment is used in over thirty countries. Salora Oy makes radio and television sets and recently concluded a deal to supply 'Finlandia' colour televisions to one of Britain's largest TV rental firms. In 1970 exports in this sector were worth £25 million ($51 million). The electricity and electronics industry has a work force of about 19,000.

The gross value of production in the manufacturing and mechanical engineering sector in 1970 was about £704 million ($1,690 million), which can be divided up as follows: manufacture of metal products £124 million ($298 million); manufacture of machinery £209 million ($502 million); manufacture of electrical machinery, etc £124 million ($298 million);

manufacture of transport equipment £192 million ($461 million), of which shipbuilding comprised 45 per cent, ie £86 million ($206 million), and other manufacturing industries in the metal sector £55 million ($132 million).

Exports totalled £183 million ($439 million) the most important groups being, as already shown, shipbuilding £62 million ($149 million); machinery £60 million ($144 million), electrotechnical £25 million ($51 million). About 160,000 workers are employed in these industries (46,000 in the transport equipment industry, 50,000 in the machinery industry).

TEXTILES AND CLOTHING

The Finnish textile industry has a tradition going back over two hundred years, but it was not until the 1820s that a cotton mill was established by a Scotsman called James Finlayson. Poor returns made Finlayson sell out in 1836, but the company bearing his name continued in operation and is today one of the leading textile concerns in the country. Other large textile manufacturers include Tampella, Barker-Littonen (also founded by a Briton) and Suomen Trikoo.

Finland's textile industry is expanding very fast in the export field, for in 1968 exports were worth £31 million ($75 million) while by 1970 the figure was double this, representing 6·5 per cent of exports. Much of this success has been due to the originality of approach of the leading Finnish designers, who have combined striking patterns with bold colours to produce fabrics which have made names such as Marimekko, Metsovaara and Vuokko synonymous with Finnish textile design in recent years. The Finns have also paid close attention to fashion in the clothing and shoes produced by firms such as Lassila and Tikanoja, Kestilä and Yhtyneet Pukutehtaat. In 1970 the gross value of production in the textile industry was £134 million ($322 million) and in the clothing and footwear sector, £108 million ($259 million). The labour forces were 30,000 and 37,000 respectively.

CERAMICS AND GLASS

If one picks up a piece of pottery in a Finnish home the chances are that one will find the trademark of the Arabia concern on the bottom. Founded on the Arabia estate outside Helsinki in 1873, the ceramics factory, which is one of the largest in the world, is now part of the Wärtsilä company, famous in shipping circles for its ice-breakers. As in other modern Finnish design, the emphasis in the pottery from the Arabia factory is on functional beauty, and the successful achievement of this aim has made Arabia products justifiably popular in Finland and many other countries. Arabia employ a number of artists who are given a free hand in designing works of art using ceramic techniques.

Wärtsilä also control the Nuutajärvi glassworks at Urjala, and other glass-making concerns include Iittala and Riihimäki glass. Although the gross value of production in these sectors is not particularly high—1970 figures, ceramics £6 million ($14 million), glass £9.5 million ($23 million)—Finnish glass and pottery is much sought after by connoisseurs of modern design. The labour force of the two industries is about 6,000.

CHEMICALS

The Finnish chemical industry is based on metal ores found in Finland and the by-products of oil-refining plants and the chemical wood-processing industry. The main exports of the chemical industry are titanium dioxide, man-made fibres and vanadium pentoxide, while other products for home use and export include soaps, fertilisers and turpentine. There is also a sizeable pharmaceutical industry preparing Finnish drugs and also foreign drugs under licence. The gross value of production in the chemical industry in 1970 was £173 million ($415 million) and in the same year the industry earned £35 million ($84 million) in exports, 3·6 per cent of total exports. About 18,000 people work in the industry.

OTHER MANUFACTURING INDUSTRIES

Other industries which make a significant contribution to the Finnish economy include the food and drinks industry, gross value of production in 1970 £728 million ($1,747 million), publishing and printing (gvp 1970 £114 million ($274 million)), manufacture of petroleum and asphalt (gvp 1970 £88 million ($211 million)), manufacture of cement, concrete and building materials (gvp 1970 £42 million ($101 million)), and plastics (gvp 1970 £39 million ($94 million)).

AGRICULTURE

While the increase in industrial production since the war has caused justifiable satisfaction among Finns, the agricultural sector has been the source of considerable concern, as recently production has been expanding at a faster rate than consumption. Following World War II many of the displaced Karelians were resettled on land which had been made available by a large-scale forest-clearance programme. Although this contributed to solving the refugee problem with commendable speed, it created a long-term problem by increasing the amount of land under cultivation. However, the resettlement of the Karelians was not the only factor, for land-clearance continued throughout the fifties and into the sixties (it is estimated that about 395,200 acres were added to the area of cultivated land in Finland between 1956 and 1966), while improved agricultural methods also contributed to increased productivity. In an effort to check this expansion the government instituted a 'land bank' scheme in 1969, under which farmers who agreed not to cultivate their fields were paid a grant calculated on the size of their farms. In the first two years of the scheme's operation over 321,000 acres were taken out of cultivation, while the size of the wheat and rye crop fell from 6·4 million tons in 1968 to about 5·3 million tons in 1970.

Although the Finns are the world champion drinkers of milk, even they have been unable to cope with the over-production of dairy products which occurred during the sixties. The existence of the *voivuori* or 'butter mountain' caused the authorities considerable embarrassment, and the situation was only relieved when butter sales were held throughout the country and some foreign countries (notably Britain) were persuaded to increase their quotas of Finnish butter.

The 230 or so dairies belonging to the Valio co-operative, established in 1905, handle 85 per cent of the milk, 90 per cent of the butter and 85 per cent of the cheese produced in Finland. In 1970 over 622 million gallons of milk were produced, 5 per cent less than in 1969, while butter production fell by 14 per cent to 190 million lb, 63 million lb of which was exported. Cheese production was 90 million lb, half of which was exported, mainly to the USA, Italy and Belgium.

Finland is not, of course, unique in facing difficulties in agriculture and indeed much of her marketing problem is due to a world surplus of dairy products. But in Finland the situation is aggravated by the fact that some 21 per cent of the labour force depend on farming to some extent, compared with 3 per cent in Britain and about 6 per cent in the United States. Any large-scale programme to reduce the number of small and inefficient farms would have grave social and economic consequences, particularly as the smallest farms are found in the economically depressed areas such as Kainuu (NE Finland) and Lappi, where the chances of alternative employment are low. In 1969 Finland had 297,257 farms, over 92 per cent of which had an arable area of under 20 hectares (49·4 acres). Over 75 per cent of the farms with an arable area exceeding 100 hectares (247 acres) were found in the three southern provinces of Uusimaa, Turku-Pori and Häme. The province of Lappi had 15,921 farms, but only 21 of these had an arable area of more than 30 hectares (74 acres). Many of the small farms lack modern equipment and tend to use methods which have been relied on for generations, but on the medium and large-sized farms mechanisation has made some progress. In 1960 the motive power on many farms came from 250,000 horses employed as draught animals; in 1971 there were under 80,000 horses and more than 170,000 tractors. Combines, milking machines and other mechanical equipment are also tending to make the lot of some farmers easier, but as we have seen earlier a large number of farms lack many basic amenities.

FISHING

There are about 2,380 full-time and a further 6,850 part-time fishermen in Finland. About 380 of the former and 2,500 of the latter operate on inland waters. The sea-fishing fleet consists of about 300 boats, most of which are used in the Gulf of Finland and the waters of the Turku archipelago. In 1969 the catch totalled 86·7 million tons, worth about £7.7 million ($18.5 million). The most important fish caught are *silakka* (Baltic herring), herring, salmon and trout.

FUEL AND POWER

As Finland possesses no coal or oil reserves the greater part of her fuel requirements must be imported. In 1970 fuel to the value of £125 million ($300 million) was imported. Fuel thus accounted for 11 per cent of all imports, a rise of 32 per cent over 1969. The largest oil concern is the state-owned Neste company which operates two oil refineries, at Naantali and Porvoo, and is planning another. In addition to being used for transport, oil is widely used for domestic and industrial heating and for the generation of electricity. In 1970 22,562 million kilowatts of electric power were generated in Finland, much of it from hydro-electric plants, especially in the north of the country. The state-controlled Imatran Voima Oy (Imatra

Power Co), which produces 47 per cent of all the electricity used in Finland, signed an agreement with Soviet V/O Techno-promexport in 1970 for a nuclear power station, to be constructed near Loviisa on the south coast. In 1971 a sister-plant was ordered from the same source, while future plans include a station using Swedish expertise.

Although mains gas has never been common in Finland, only a few towns having had gas-making plants, which are now being run down, bottled gas is used extensively in country areas and in summer cottages. In April 1971 an agreement for the supply of natural gas, for use in industry, was signed with the Soviet Union. The agreement runs for twenty years, with imports beginning in 1974. In the first year 500 million cubic metres will be supplied, and the amount will increase annually, up to 1,400 million cubic metres in 1979.

FOREIGN TRADE

As a country with a few raw materials and a restricted domestic market Finland is acutely aware of the importance of foreign trade. In 1970 the total value of Finland's exports was £964 million ($2,314 million), that is about £205 ($492) per head of population, compared with £142 ($341) per head for the United Kingdom and £87 ($209) for the United States. In the same year imports totalled £1,101 million ($2,642 million), about £233 ($559) per head UK £159 ($382), USA £75 ($180).

It has already been mentioned that forestry products play the most important part in Finland's export trade, but whereas the share of paper and allied products has remained relatively stable for over twenty years, in 1949 their share was 39·7 per cent, in 1970 39·1 per cent; that of wood products has declined from 48·3 per cent in 1949 to 16·8 per cent in 1970. During this twenty-one-year period the contribution of the metal industries to exports has risen from a mere 4·3 per cent to over 25 per cent.

Raw materials comprise Finland's largest import group

(44·4 per cent in 1970), followed by investment goods (26·2 per cent) and consumer goods (18·1 per cent). The most important raw materials are those destined for the metal manufacturing industry, while there is also considerable import of materials for use in the chemical and textile industries. In other categories imports range from cars and other motor vehicles (which with spares make up the most important group of imports among consumer goods) to machinery, clothing and foodstuffs. (As mentioned earlier, fuels made up 11 per cent of all imports in 1970.)

In 1938 the United Kingdom bought over 44 per cent of Finland's exports and was also the country's largest supplier, with 21·6 per cent of the Finnish market. Germany was Finland's second largest trading partner at that time, supplying Finland with 20 per cent of her needs, and taking 14·8 per cent of Finnish exports. Sweden's contribution to Finland's imports was 12·9 per cent; she also took 4·8 per cent of Finland's exports. At that time the Soviet Union played an insignificant part in Finland's trade, receiving 0·5 per cent of Finland's exports and supplying only 1·2 per cent of imports.

In 1970 Britain was still Finland's most important customer, taking 17·7 per cent of exports, but was only in third place when imports are considered, supplying 15·7 per cent, compared with Sweden's 17·3 per cent and West Germany's 17 per cent. In 1970 Sweden took 15·9 per cent and West Germany 10·6 per cent of Finland's exports. Following the most-favoured nation clause included in the 1947 trade agreement between Finland and the USSR trade between the two countries expanded rapidly, and in 1970 the Soviet Union was Finland's fourth largest trade partner, taking 11·9 per cent of Finland's exports and supplying 12·5 per cent of her imports. In 1970 the United States took 4·7 per cent of Finland's exports, while imports from the USA amounted to 4·4 per cent of Finland's total. Finland has been an associate member of EFTA since March 1961, and in 1970 44·5 per cent of all exports went to EFTA countries. This compares with 23·3 per cent of exports to EEC countries and 15·8 per cent to members of the Eastern Bloc.

EFTA is also important as far as imports are concerned, for in 1970 over 44 per cent of Finnish imports came from EFTA countries, 27·8 per cent from members of the EEC, and a further 16·2 per cent from the Eastern Bloc.

During the second half of the sixties discussions took place between Finland and the other Nordic countries about the possibility of forming an inter-Nordic trading group—Nordek. The talks broke down in 1969, largely due to Finland's sudden unwillingness to commit herself to such a union in the light of possible political implications affecting her relations with the Soviet Union.

Finland's position in regard to the EEC is unclear at the present time. Now Britain has joined the community two of Finland's leading trade partners, Britain and West Germany, are members of an economic union from which she is excluded by her unwillingness to compromise her neutrality and the problems of a probable negative reaction to such a move from the USSR. It is acknowledged by virtually all Finnish politicians, from President Kekkonen down, that membership of the EEC is not a practical proposition, but agreement has been reached with the community about special arrangements for Finland. Discussions have also taken place with the socialist countries about the development of trade between Finland and the East. Finland once again seems to be suffering from the fact that she is caught between two groups who regard each other with mutual suspicion. In such a position there is little alternative but for her to declare bravely that as a neutral country she does not wish to get involved with either side but remain on good terms with both.

CONTROL OF INDUSTRY AND THE MEANS OF PRODUCTION

As far as ownership of the means of production is concerned Finland can be described as a mixed economy, with a strong bias towards private enterprise. Practically the whole of agriculture, 99 per cent, and 85 per cent of forestry is in private hands, as is 86 per cent of manufacturing industry, 96 per cent of housing construction and 86 per cent of banking and insurance. The state tends to be involved in enterprises requiring a large amount of initial capital, such as mining; basic industries, for example iron and steel production; and, as in many other countries, the transport and communications industries. The state is responsible for 80 per cent of the mining in Finland, the largest company being Outokumpu Oy, originally set up between the wars to exploit the copper in the Outokumpu area of eastern Finland. The iron and steel plants of Rautaruukki Oy produce 64 per cent of Finland's steel, while another important state-owned company in the basic industry sector is Neste Oy, which controls the largest oil refinery in the Nordic countries.

Nationalisation is not really a political issue in Finland and in many cases state-owned firms are in competition with private enterprise, a notable exception being Oy Alko Ab, which holds an absolute monopoly of the sale of alcohol. A company is considered to be state-owned if more than half the shares are owned by the state or by another state-owned company. Finland's two largest industrial companies, Neste and Enso-Gutzeit Oy (paper, wood, chemicals and engineering) are both state-controlled. It is estimated that state-controlled companies are responsible for about 17 per cent of industrial production and just over 20 per cent of exports; they employ 59,124 workers.

It will have been noticed that many Finnish business concerns have the prefix or suffix *Oy* or *Ab*, and in some cases both. *Oy* is the abbreviation of *osakeyhtiö*, and *Ab* of *aktiebolag*, respectively the Finnish and Swedish equivalents of 'Co Ltd' or 'Inc'. The joint stock company is the most important form of private enterprise organisation in Finland, but partnerships, limited liability partnerships and co-operatives can also be found, the last-mentioned being quite common in wholesale and retail trading.

BANKING AND FINANCE

Finland's central bank, which is also the sole bank of issue, is the Bank of Finland (*Suomen Pankki*) established in 1811. It is an autonomous public institution operating under parliamentary supervision, which is exercised by a board appointed by the *eduskunta*. The day-to-day running of the bank is in the hands of the board of management, the members of whom are chosen by the President of the Republic.

Finland has seven commercial banks, though in practice something like 70 per cent of the business is done by the two largest, Kansallis-Osake-Pankki, founded in 1889, which has over 400 branches, and Pohjoismaiden Yhdyspankki, founded in 1862, with some 340 branches. The commercial banks tend to dominate foreign business, but in all other branches of banking they compete with the savings banks (*säästöpankit*), the co-operative banks (*osuuspankit*) and the Post Office Bank (*Postipankki*). Savings banks were originally very numerous, being established in country areas to serve the needs of the communes. Since World War II there have been many amalgamations, a trend that is still continuing, but there are still over 300 banks, with more than a thousand branches. *Säästöpankkien Keskus-Osake-Pankki*, the central bank of the savings banks, is considered to be a commercial bank. The majority of co-operative banks were originally farmers' credit societies, but they have extended their activities to include virtually every branch of banking business; the co-operative banks number about 440.

In terms of deposits *Postipankki* is the third largest bank in the country. The bank was founded as *Postisäästöpankki* (The Post Office Savings Bank) in 1886, and its business began to expand significantly after the introduction of the *postisiirto* (giro) in October 1939. *Postipankki* is administered separately from the Post Office, but conducts the majority of its business activities through the post office network, which means that, including individual post offices, it has the largest number of branches in the country, a total of 2,911.

The Mortgage Bank of Finland was established in 1956 to channel loans from the World Bank and other foreign institutions to Finnish industry. Recently, however, the Mortgage Bank has been reorganised, and it will now provide capital for industrial operations requiring large sums of money. Other important financial institutions in Finland include the National Pensions Institute, the sixty-two private insurance companies, Teollistamisrahasto Oy (Industrialisation Fund Ltd), a privately controlled development bank, Vientiluotto Oy (Export Credit Ltd) which grants credit for export, and Sponsor Oy.

The most important credit-granting institutions are the commercial banks, followed by the savings banks, the insurance companies and the co-operative banks. One of the greatest problems facing Finland since the war has been the shortage of capital, and the private sector in particular has often been starved of finance. Until recently the tax laws made it more advantageous for firms to use external capital rather than attempt to increase their own, and this was reflected in the somnolence of the country's only stock exchange (*pörssi*) in Helsinki. In 1950 the turnover of the Helsinki Stock Exchange was 29·6 million marks, in 1960 26·3 million marks and in 1966 29·3 million marks. Revision of the tax laws, however, stimulated new business, and in 1971 turnover had increased to 92·5 million marks.

EMPLOYMENT AND UNEMPLOYMENT

As is the case in many other countries Finland's unemployment problem is a regional one, unemployment being worse in the north, particularly in Lappi, and the east, than in more southerly areas.

At present Finland is suffering from an acute shortage of skilled labour in industry, and this has been accentuated by the large-scale migration to Sweden, where wages are higher. Recently attempts have been made to woo some of these workers back, and an official has been seconded to the Finnish Embassy in Stockholm to assist Finns who wish to return home. It is also thought, and hoped, that in the last few years the number of Finns leaving to take up permanent residence in Sweden has decreased.

In 1970 3,492,000 of the population were aged 15 (the official school-leaving age) or over. It is estimated that some 1,298,000 or 37 per cent of these were not available as part of the labour force as they were still at school or in other full-time education. This means that the effective Finnish labour force, in 1970, was 2,194,000. Of these 2,153,000 were employed, giving an unemployment rate of 1·9 per cent, compared with 2·8 per cent in 1969 and 4 per cent the year before. In 1972 the unemployment rate was 2·6 per cent.

Women play an active part in economic life in Finland; in 1970 it was estimated that 36 per cent of the labour force in industry were women. In towns every other woman goes out to work, while in rural areas the figure is one in every five. Nearly half the students at Finnish universities are women, and many of these later become doctors, dentists and teachers, though

Lapland—Pallastunturi, 2,647ft

Skolt woman

women are also prominent in business, especially in retailing. Most of the barbers in the country are women, as are the majority of bank clerks and shop assistants. Women are also active in politics, at both local and national level, as might be expected in a country where women were given political rights at the beginning of the century. In 1971 the first woman *maaherra* (governor) was appointed, while in early 1972 a Finnish woman became an assistant Secretary General at the United Nations.

INDUSTRIAL RELATIONS

The Finnish trade union movement was started in the second half of the nineteenth century, and in 1907 the forerunner of Suomen Ammattiliittojen Keskusjärjestö—SAK—the equivalent of the British TUC was founded. Today SAK has a membership of over 700,000 workers. Other union organisations include TVK, which represents salaried staffs and civil servants, with about 221,000 members, AKAVA, whose members are drawn from professional organisations, for

———

Reindeer round-up in Finnish Lapland

Lapp transport old and new

example university teachers, doctors, priests and army officers, and a number of smaller federations.

On the employers' side the largest organisation is Suomen Työnantajain Keskusliitto—STK—which has about thirty members. Liiketyönantajain Keskusliitto—LK—is restricted to commercial organisations such as banks and insurance companies, while Maaseudun Työnantajaliitto—MTL—represents employers in agriculture and the forestry industry.

Since the last war collective agreements between unions and management have become widespread. Such agreements are made for a definite period, not exceeding four years, or until further notice. In practice most agreements are discussed, and if necessary amended, after one or two years. Once an agreement has been concluded, both sides are expected to honour it and refrain from any action that might infringe its provisions. Any employer or employee who offends must pay compensation to the injured party. Disputes over collective agreements and their interpretation are heard in the Labour Court (*Työtuomioistuin*), the members of which are appointed by the President of the Republic for three years. The chairman of the court and two of the assessors are officially neutral, while three assessors are nominated by the employers' federations and three by the unions. Decisions of the Labour Court are final, and there is no possibility of appeal.

In addition to the Labour Court there is a Labour Council (*Työneuvosto*), the function of which is to investigate matters in the field of employee protection and to advise a court of law should such a case be brought before it. Although decisions and recommendations made by the Labour Council do not carry the force of law, they are nevertheless important as guidelines. Further protection of workers is ensured by a government-appointed inspectorate, which covers all areas of industrial activity.

A key figure in Finnish industrial relations is the National Conciliation Officer (*valtakunnansovittelija*) who, with his assistants, acts or attempts to act as a mediator between employers and workers in the event of industrial disputes. Should workers be planning a strike—or employers a lock-out—they must give at least two weeks' notice of the intended action to those affected and to the Conciliation Officer. Thus it is quite common to see newspaper headlines announcing *lakko* (a strike) which is planned to begin in two weeks' time. Arbitration is encouraged during the period before a strike but is not compulsory, and if they choose both sides can sit and wait for the strike to come about, taking no action other than ticking off the days on the calendar. In practice, however, in the majority of cases both sides get together in order to see if they can avert the threatened stoppage. Out of a total of 240 strikes in 1970 205 were solved by a compromise, in 18 cases the employers' terms were accepted, while in 9 cases the workers were successful.

5

How They Learn

THE Finns have always had a high regard for education, and as early as 1683 a proposal was made that primary education should be provided for the entire population. One result was the religious law of 1686 which declared that it was the duty of every citizen to learn to read. In an attempt to make the law effective the Church refused to confirm or marry those who were illiterate, a stand which not surprisingly produced a sharp rise in the rate of literacy. A British naval officer who came into contact with Finns during the Baltic campaign of 1854 wrote home, 'It is certainly not creditable to us as a nation that we should be so behind in education those we have previously considered half-barbarous Finns. They can hardly believe that numbers of people in England cannot read.'

Although literacy might have been high in Finland during the nineteenth century, until the late 1850s secondary education remained the prerogative of the Swedish-speaking members of the population. In 1858, however, a secondary school giving instruction in Finnish was established in the town of Jyväskylä, and proved to be such a success that other schools were set up on similar lines. By the 1890s each school district was expected to provide a primary school for children in the area, though it was not until 1921 that school attendance became compulsory.

SCHOOLS

In recent years there has been much discussion about the type of school most suited to Finland's future needs, and a great deal of attention has been paid to the systems used in other countries, particularly Sweden. It was decided to introduce a system based on the comprehensive school (*peruskoulu*), and in July 1968 the *eduskunta* passed an act providing for the introduction of comprehensive schools throughout the country. The act came into force in 1970, and the first *peruskoulut* (apart from a number of experimental institutions) are being established in the north of the country. The system is gradually being extended southwards, until by 1980 it is hoped that the old schools will be entirely replaced by comprehensive schools.

Under the old system, still in force in many parts of the country, children enter the primary school at the age of seven, and at eleven some take an examination for entrance to the secondary school. Children who pass the examination go to the junior secondary school (*keskikoulu*) for five years, and then may go on to the senior secondary school (*lukio*) for a further three. In practice many secondary schools have the two stages under one roof, the whole being known as *oppikoulu*. Children who do not take, or who fail, the examination at eleven, remain in the *kansakoulu* for a further two years, and then go to a 'civic school' (*kansalaiskoulu*) for a further two years, leaving at fifteen, the official school-leaving age. Pupils attending secondary school either leave at sixteen, after *keskikoulu*, or stay on in the *lukio* to prepare for the student examination (*ylioppilastutkinto*), which is taken at eighteen or nineteen. Success in the *ylioppilastutkinto* is important academically—it is the initial qualification for entry into higher education—and socially, too. Upon hearing that he or she has passed the examination the newly qualified *ylioppilas* (student) acquires a white cap with a lyre badge and a large bunch of roses. Armed with these signs of a new status the student then visits the photographer, so that visible proof of graduation may be displayed on the family sideboard.

It seems, however, that soon the tradition of the white cap, originally imported from Germany along with other features of that country's education system many years ago, will soon die out, as the new school system will probably do away with the student examination, at least in its present form. In the *peru-skoulu* all children will start at the same school at the age of seven and receive a standard schooling for nine years. At the age of sixteen pupils will have the option of leaving school or continuing their education in the *lukio*, which will thus be a kind of sixth-form college, giving a general education, and also preparing pupils for higher education. The question of what will happen to the student examination has not yet been resolved. Some feel that it should be abolished, leaving the universities to set their own entrance tests, while others feel that it should be retained, as some kind of school-leaving examination is necessary.

Under the old system, fees of about £6 ($15) a term are charged in state schools at the secondary level, while fees at private schools would be up to twice as much. However, fees have been abolished in comprehensive schools, so in the future secondary education, like that at the primary level, will be free.

Schools, like all other educational institutions in Finland, come under the control of the Ministry of Education (*opetus-ministeriö*). The organisation of school education is largely in the hands of *Kouluhallitus* (The National Board of Schools) which has far-reaching powers of intervention and control. Although centralisation of education may have advantages, in that it is possible to have a uniform system and therefore similar standards over the whole of the country, the great power exercised by *Kouluhallitus* (it decides on teaching methods, syllabuses and which books can be used in schools) means that on occasion individual initiative can be restricted. It seems likely that before very long the position of *Kouluhallitus* and its relationship to the Ministry of Education will be reviewed.

HIGHER EDUCATION

The first university in Finland was founded in 1640 in Turku (Swedish Åbo). The first *Åbo Akademi* was, of course, a Swedish language institution, and it retained this language when it moved to the new capital of Helsinki, following the Great Fire of Turku, in 1828. Towards the end of the nineteenth century a move away from Swedish began as a result of the nationalist movement, and today the University of Helsinki (*Helsingin Yliopisto*) is a bi-lingual institution, a certain proportion of the staff and students being Swedish-speaking. The rapid increase in the number of Finnish-speaking staff and students at the university worried the Swedish-Finns, and in 1917 they founded a Swedish-language university in Turku, the second *Åbo Akademi*. Three years later the Finnish University of Turku (*Turun Yliopisto*) was established, the first university in which Finnish was the only official language. Since then a number of other universities have been set up, at Tampere, Jyväskylä and Oulu (until 1972 the northernmost university in the world) and at the end of the sixties Joensuu and Kuopio.

The university (*yliopisto*), however, is not the only institution of higher education in Finland. The generic name for establishments offering degree-level courses is *korkeakoulu* (high school) and at the present time there are eighteen of these. In addition to the universities there are five schools of economics and business administration, three of which are for Finnish-speakers, two for Swedish-speakers, three institutes of technology, a veterinary college, and the Sibelius Academy for students of music.

In 1966 there were about 46,000 students studying at institutes of higher education; at the end of 1971 the figure was 59,634, 47·2 per cent of them being women. In 1971, out of the 20,669 pupils who took the student examination, 19,892, that is 96·2 per cent, passed, thus qualifying for university entrance, but, as in many other countries, demand far exceeds supply and a large number were unsuccessful in getting places.

It is interesting to note that Finland has more professors than any of the other Nordic countries (in 1969/70 the figures were as follows: Finland 1,020, Sweden 917, Norway 402, Denmark 613, and fewer staff at other levels (with the exception of Norway, which in 1969/70 had 27,483 students, compared with 57,299 in Finland), viz, Finland 2,510, Sweden 4,980, Norway

2,012, Denmark 3,014. Whereas in Britain there are nearly 9 other staff members to each professor, in Finland the ratio of other staff to professors is 2·2 to one. As might be expected the staff-student ratio is also very different. In British university-level institutions have a member of staff for every 8 students, in Finland the figure is about 18 students for each staff member. The inevitable result is that there is very little contact between staff and students, the latter being left much to their own devices, while in teaching the emphasis tends to be on lectures followed by examinations, rather than on classes and tutorials. It might be argued that this situation develops the capacity of the student to work unsupervised, but in fact the opposite usually occurs, and many of the students, who are faced with a very heavy work-load as they are expected to study three subjects, are unable to make the best use of their time. Lack of discussion and guidance means that, although the students can acquire a great deal of information from books, they are unable to apply what they have learnt, as only too often the only chance which they have to use their knowledge is when answering examination questions.

A survey of Finnish students carried out by SYL (Suomen Ylioppilaskuntien Liitto—The National Union of Finnish Students) in 1966 found that the majority of Finnish students were in the age-range 20 to 25, only 10 per cent were under 20, while 29 per cent were over 25. The high average age of Finnish students, compared to those in the USA or Britain, is partly due to the fact that whereas virtually all first-degree courses at English universities (apart from subjects like medicine) last for three years, the average Finn studies for five or six years and sometimes even longer. There are very few scholarships in Finland, and students must finance their studies through loans, parental assistance or their own earnings. During the academic year 1971/72 about 65 per cent of the students in higher education received student loans. The interest on these loans, which are available from banks, was 6¾ per cent, 3 per cent of which was paid by the student, the rest by the state. Students also get other benefits such as reduced fares between their home and the town where they are studying, cheap cinema and theatre tickets, and in some cases subsidised housing.

Many students get married after being at university for two or three years and then continue their studies, often taking a part-time job to supplement the family income. According to the 1966 survey about 19 per cent of female students and 25 per cent male students were married.

Possibly because this sizeable minority of the students are married and have children, so that their interests tend to lie outside the university, there are not the large number of societies and organisations that are characteristic of British and American student life. Another reason undoubtedly is that Finnish universities are, for the most part, non-residential; under 14 per cent of unmarried students and only about 5 per cent of married students live in halls of residence. In the older institutions social life used to be concentrated in the 'Student Nations' (*Ylioppilaskunnat*) to which all students from the same area belonged, and which provided them with a home-from-home at the university. This system, however, seems to be losing support; at the newer institutions they do not exist, while at the older universities those students interested in participating in university life tend to join faculty organisations or political clubs.

In recent years certain groups among the students have been pressing for more say in the running of their universities. In 1968 it was suggested that a 'tripartite principle' should be introduced, so that the membership of the decision-making body of each university would consist of one-third professors, one-third junior teachers and one-third students. Not surprisingly the senior members of the universities were not prepared to accept this, and student opinion, or at least a vocal section of it, moved in favour of one man, one vote. In 1969 it became clear that the government had accepted the principle, and in March 1970 a bill was introduced by the Minister of Education which would have given one man, one vote. However it was not possible to get the bill through before the end of the session, so the measure lapsed, and with it the opportunity of seeing the

Finnish high schools changing from professor-dominated to 'democratic' institutions overnight. Another interesting feature of the controversy was to see how much power of interference in the internal affairs of the university the state possesses. A number of the higher education institutions are state-controlled, while others rely on state funds for the greater part of their income. Whereas in Britain and the United States universities tend to take a pride in their individuality, frequently—especially in Britain—taking it to absurd lengths, all Finnish universities are organised on basically similar lines, with Helsinki as the model. It is significant that the Chancellor of the University of Helsinki is consulted on matters concerning the universities even if Helsinki is not directly affected.

The degrees awarded by Finnish universities are rather different from those given in Britain and the USA, and are not directly comparable. Thus in the Faculties of Arts there are four levels: *Humanististen tieteiden kandidaatti* (*HuK*) an intermediate degree, *Filosofian kandidaatti* (*FK*) or final degree, *Filosofian lisensiaatti* (*FL*) an intermediate degree, which is taken before *Filosofian tohtori* (*FT*) the Finnish equivalent of the British or American PhD, while the degrees in other faculties correspond to these.

Finnish universities have only two terms, one in the autumn, the other in the spring; thus the academic year runs from the beginning of September to mid-May. But at most universities there is a separate summer session, known as the *kesäyliopisto* (summer university). The *kesäyliopisto* is unique to Finland and is designed to give crash courses of four or five weeks for students, teachers and others who are interested in improving their qualifications. There are about nineteen of these summer universities each year, many of them run by non-university establishments, though they are usually staffed by university teachers; they are attended by some 30,000 students.

There are also a large number of other institutions providing vocational training at various levels. The five *kieli-instituutit* (language institutes), which can be considered to give university-level teaching, train specialist interpreters in a number of different fields. There are also schools for nurses, public health employees, agriculturalists, seamen and others, while virtually every town of any size will have a *teknillinen opisto* (technical college) or at least an *ammattikoulu* (trade school). The *kauppakoulut* and *kauppaopistot* (commercial schools and institutes) give business courses and also train secretaries.

There are also about eighty folk high schools (*kansanopistot*) which provide residential courses for about 8,000 pupils, mostly women, so that they can go on to higher studies if they wish. The workers' evening institutes (*työväenopistot*) arrange courses on a variety of subjects, from foreign languages to china painting; these are attended by over 200,000 people, being particularly popular in the dark winter months. Both the *kansanopistot* and the *työväenopistot* are assisted from state and communal funds.

6

How They Get About

THE responsibility for providing public transport in Finland is divided between state and private concerns. Railways, the majority of air traffic and some bus lines are operated by the state or municipal undertakings, while the bulk of road transport is in private hands. In 1970 the transport and communications sector represented 7 per cent of the net national product and employed 149,000 people, 7 per cent of the total labour force.

In 1955 buses accounted for 41 per cent of domestic passenger transport, the railways for 27 per cent; in 1969 the figures were 20 per cent and 7 per cent respectively. Over the same period the contribution of private cars has risen from 26 per cent to 68 per cent. In both 1955 and 1969 the share of aircraft was a mere 1 per cent. As far as the transport of freight is concerned there has been a movement away from the railways and 'floating' (of timber) in favour of motor lorries and, to a lesser extent, ships. In 1955 lorries and vans accounted for 26 per cent of freight traffic, compared with 48 per cent for the railways, in 1968 58 per cent of goods went by road, 28 per cent by rail. In 1955 only 1 per cent of domestic traffic was carried in ships, by 1969 the figure had risen to 6 per cent, while floating dropped from 25 per cent in 1955 to 8 per cent in 1969.

RAILWAYS

In 1970 *Suomen Valtion Rautatiet* (*VR*)—Finnish State Railways —operated a rail network of some 3,620 miles, just over 300 miles of which were double track. Faced with strong competition from road transport the railways have tried to keep transport costs low, and in 1971 charges for both goods and passengers were lower than for any other Nordic country. A single ticket for a journey of 50 kilometres (31 miles) cost £0.29 ($0.69) in Finland, compared with £0.60 ($1.44) in Norway and £0.82 ($1.96) in Sweden, while goods rates show a similar pattern. Nevertheless this has not prevented the railways from losing traffic to other forms of transport, and has presumably contributed towards their losing money: in 1970 *Valtion Rautatiet's* deficit was £11.8 million ($28.3 million), £3 million ($7.20 million) more than in 1969. Between 1969 and 1970 the amount of freight carried by the railways increased by 50 per cent, but passenger traffic declined, particularly on local services, where there were estimated to be 20 per cent fewer travellers in 1970 than there had been the previous year.

When David Lean shot the railway sequences for the film of *Dr Zhivago* he enlisted the assistance of VR, and a few years ago one might have been excused for thinking that the passenger-stock in general use had been left over from the film. However romantic the old wooden coaches looked when they stood, wreathed in steam and festooned with icicles, on a winter's evening under the clock of Saarinen's great railway station in Helsinki, a journey in one of them could be extremely uncomfortable. Many had hard wooden seats, while during the winter heating was provided by a large wood-fired stove, which either fought a losing battle with draughts from doors and windows, or else heated the coach so efficiently that it was turned into a sauna on wheels. Now virtually all the old stock has been condemned, to be replaced with low-slung all-metal coaches with efficient heating, comfortable seats and plenty of luggage space.

The orange-and-white three-car motor units that link Helsinki and the leading provincial centres are equal, if not superior, to passenger stock elsewhere in the world, having aircraft-type adjustable seats, automatically closing doors and a public-address system. One of the drawbacks of the Finnish railway system is that journeys tend to be extremely time-consuming. Whereas in many countries, for example Britain, rail scores over road transport because it is faster, and over air because it goes from city centre to city centre, in Finland trains tend to be slow, while the tracks often follow a circuitous route. Thus the line from eastern Finland enters Helsinki from the north, while to travel from Turku to Vaasa by train involves going by way of Tampere.

In 1970 there were 373 railway stations in Finland but, as in Britain, a large number of stations have been declared redundant, 150 having closed down between 1966 and 1971. Although stations have been closed, the length of track-mileage is still increasing, and in June 1971 a new line was opened between Tampere and Seinäjoki, which considerably reduces travelling time between Helsinki and the north. In 1970 the staff of *Valtion Rautatiet* was 28,100.

The first train in Finland ran between Helsinki and Hämeenlinna in 1861. As Finland was at that time part of the Russian Empire the track was constructed to the Russian broad guage of 5 feet. As all subsequent main lines were the same guage it has not been possible to develop satisfactory rail communications between Finland and the west, though there are facilities for transferring rail freight at the Swedish/Finnish border at the head of the Gulf of Bothnia. There is also a train ferry operating across the south of the Gulf from Naantali which carried 130,000 tons of goods in 1969. The rail link between Finland and the Soviet Union, however, is of considerably greater importance, and it is estimated that 4 million tons of material cross the eastern border every year by rail. Container traffic has been increasing in recent years, and some Finnish railwaymen have been speculating on the chances of Finland becoming an international railway junction for goods brought overland from

Japan. Containers have already been sent to Finland by means of the Trans-Siberian railway, taking 25–30 days, compared with the 60 or more taken by a ship on the Cape route.

ROADS

Finland has a road network of about 44,640 miles, about half a mile for every square mile of land. The USA has 1 mile of road for every square mile of land, the United Kingdom 2¼ miles. Although it is claimed that over 32 per cent of Finnish roads are surfaced, in practice only about 11·5 per cent are coated with tarmacadam or similar hard surface; the remaining 20·5 per cent are covered with oil-gravel, the purpose of which seems to be to conceal stones from the driver until it is too late. About 68 per cent of Finnish roads are completely unsurfaced, the only attention they receive being a periodic levelling by the road department's machines, or a visit from a road gang who fill in the worst of the potholes. Even the metalled roads are often in indifferent condition, owing to the action of ice and the amount of heavy traffic they have to carry. In 1969 the state spent a total of £66.6 million ($159.8 million) on various aspects of road construction and maintenance. According to a survey of road expenditure published in *The Economist*, in the United Kingdom 42 per cent and in the United States 86 per cent of road tax was actually spent on the roads; the figure for Finland was 128 per cent (though in Finland there is no annual licence tax).

In 1970 there were 711,968 cars registered in Finland, that is one for every eight people. In Britain the figure is one for every five and in the United States one for every two. In terms of cars per road mile Finland has 15 cars for every mile of road, Britain has 65 and the United States 17. The great majority of Finnish cars are imported, and in 1971 the most popular car in terms of sales was the Fiat 600. The 'top ten' cars in 1971 included one German, two British, one Russian, two Swedish, two Japanese and two Italian models. The favourite prestige cars are the Volvo and Mercedes, and almost any recent American model.

For most Finns a car is not merely a means of getting from one place to another, but a way of expressing his personality. To permit another car, particularly a smaller one, to overtake is a reflection on his masculinity, while the traffic rule 'Give way to traffic coming from the right' means that an impromptu game of 'chicken' develops at nearly every intersection. It is perhaps the attitude to driving that has led to an increase of 25 per cent in fatal accidents between 1960 and 1968, but another factor has undoubtedly been the sheer growth in the number of vehicles on the road, an increase of 170 per cent over the same period. In 1970 there were 44,139 motor-cycles and mopeds registered, nor has the humble bicycle been forgotten, for it is estimated that about 150,000 of these machines are in regular use.

In 1971 there were 535 private bus companies in Finland, in addition to the state-owned *Pohjolan Liikenne* and the post buses operated by the Post Office. Inter-city and rural bus routes cover 40,300 miles, from the Turku archipelago to Utsjoki in the north of Lappi. The largest bus company is that started by the Post Office in 1921 which now has over 400 buses, operates 223 routes and carries 10 million passengers over 24 million miles a year. Long-distance buses are as a rule fast and comfortable, with ample luggage space and a conductress who seems anxious to emulate her cousin on the airlines, supplying newspapers, cold drinks and details of arrival and departure of the bus at each stage of the journey. The three largest towns have municipal traffic systems. Taxis provide a useful and relatively inexpensive supplement to public transport in both town and country areas.

There were 46,195 motor lorries and 56,707 vans registered in Finland in 1970, and as has already been mentioned they made a considerable contribution to the transport of goods within Finland. In recent years with the development of 'roll-on, roll-off' ferries they have also become important on international routes and there are regular ferries between Finland

and Sweden, Germany and Denmark all of which carry trucks. In early 1972 a lorry ferry began operations between Turku and Harwich. During 1970 79,826 lorries passed through the customs, carrying over a million tons of exports, a 37 per cent increase over 1969.

SHIPPING

Of the 16 large square-riggers still trading in the world in 1936, 12 were sailing under the Finnish flag, according to W. L. A. Derby's *The Tall Ships Pass*. Today none of these ships remains in service, though *Pommern* is permanently moored in Mariehamn as a museum; the present-day Finnish merchant marine is largely made up of modern motor ships. In March 1972 the Finnish merchant navy consisted of 484 ships, 432 of which were motor powered, a total of 1,552,696 registered tons. There are still a few of the once numerous trading schooners, but most have been converted to power; the small number that retain sails only spread them occasionally to assist the engines.

While a large number of Finland's ships are built in her own shipyards, recent additions to the Finnish fleet have come from Britain, West Germany, France and Bulgaria. In 1970 18,052 ships, 8,861 of which were Finnish, entered Finnish ports, carrying 20,180,000 tons of imports. In the same year 18,046 vessels (8,816 of them Finnish) carrying 12,360,000 tons of exports were cleared. The majority of Finland's important harbours are in the south of the country; in 1970 73·3 per cent of exports and 89·4 per cent of imports passed through the harbours between Hamina in the Gulf of Finland and Pori in the south of the Gulf of Bothnia. As the Baltic freezes in winter a fleet of powerful ice-breakers is available to keep the leading ports, such as Sköldvik, Helsinki, Kotka, Hamina and Turku, open all the year round.

In 1955 'floating' accounted for 25 per cent of all domestic transport, in 1969 for only 8 per cent. Nevertheless in 1969 20 per cent of the timber used in factories and mills was floated for an average distance of 115 miles. The development of land

H

transport, the relatively high loss when timber is carried by water and the establishment of hydro-electric schemes, which block the waterways, have all meant a decline in the importance of waterways, and this trend will probably continue.

Rivers have been used for the transport of other goods besides timber, and at one time it was a considerable tourist attraction to ride in the tar-boats of the Oulujoki. But as many of Finland's rivers are fast-flowing and have frequent rapids they are of limited value for transport on a large scale. In some places canals have been built to link up the lake systems, and the most famous Finnish canal is undoubtedly that which links Lake Saimaa with the Gulf of Finland. The Saimaa Canal was originally built in 1856 and was used until World War II. After the war much of the canal and its outlet to the sea was in Russian hands, but following discussions the Finns signed an agreement with the USSR by which they agreed to reconstruct the waterway and pay an annual rent for its use. The new canal was opened in 1968, and in 1970 129,357 tons were carried by ships using the waterway. Although this represents a 60 per cent rise over 1969 it is still a long way from the 1,038,730 tons carried in 1923, the peak year of the old canal. Many consider that the rebuilding of the canal was economically unjustified, particularly as ice restricts its use between November and May, and these critics suggest that political motives were more important than economic ones when Finland agreed to rent the canal from the Russians. Many of the lakes have passenger vessels, which range from old double-decker steam boats through modern diesels to a hydrofoil which links Lahti and Jyväskylä. In 1971 there were 41 vessels of 19 tons and over registered for use on Finland's internal waterways.

AIR TRAFFIC

Finland is not a member of the Scandinavian Airways System but runs her own national state-controlled airline, founded as Aero Oy in 1923 and now better known as Finnair. In 1971

Finnair and its subsidiary Kar-Air had a fleet of 3 DC 8-62s, 3 DC 6s, 8 Super Caravelles, 4 DC 9s and 9 Convair Metropolitans. Finnair flies to 23 cities in 16 countries, including Moscow, New York and London, and also operates a domestic network between 16 provincial centres. There are also a number of smaller companies specialising in charter work. In 1970 Finnish air lines flew 12·3 million miles and carried 1,279,538 passengers. In 1970 there was a total of 249 aircraft and 206 gliders in the country.

7

How They Amuse Themselves

WHEN one considers that during the Finnish winter the temperature can remain below − 20° C (4° F) for several weeks, it is not surprising that the promise of summer is greeted with some enthusiasm, and thus 1 May, traditionally the first day of spring, known as *vappu* in Finnish, is kept as a national holiday which is celebrated with great enthusiasm. This is not to say, of course, that the Finn does not get the most out of winter; he is a realist and takes full advantage of the fact that the snow turns the whole of the country into a vast ski-track for several months of the year. Nevertheless at the back of his mind the Finn is probably thinking about the time when the snow will disappear, the days will grow longer and it will no longer be necessary to don a heavy coat and fur hat when venturing outside. Not all Finns would go as far as the girl who said, 'Up to Christmas we think of the summer that has passed, after Christmas we are planning for the summer that is to come,' but they would understand her feelings.

The contrast between winter and summer makes Finland a country with a split personality, and this is reflected in the lives of the Finns themselves. The long, cold, hard winter is for long hours of work, a time for serious activity, while during the summer the pressure tends to be relaxed and life is taken more easily. Summer vacations for schools and universities are long, while many concerns, including government offices, go over to a five-day week during the summer, so that all can benefit from a long weekend. The crowded roads on Friday evenings throughout the summer, as town dwellers head for their cottages, show that many take advantage of the shortened week.

It is probably the ambition of most Finns to have a summer cottage (*kesämökki*), though the motives for wanting it may be complex. For many the *kesämökki* is a place where they can forget their cramped town flat and the neighbours who complain about any noise after 10 pm, and become backwoodsmen for a few days. Others look upon their summer residence as an investment or status symbol, while for large families the cottage or villa provides a summer meeting-place at weekends and for important summer occasions such as *Juhannus* (Midsummer). Many summer cottages are little more than weekend retreats, where their owners can enjoy the experience of living primitively for a short time, but others, especially those near towns, are well-appointed, with electricity, telephone and mains drainage, and are used as the family home throughout the summer. In May the family will shut up the town flat and move out to the country, only to return when the nights start drawing in, in late August or September. There are about 170,000 summer places in Finland, one for every sixth family. Although predominantly a middle and upper-class phenomenon, members of lower income groups frequently have access to cottages through their place of work, trade union or sports organisation.

The favourite site for a summer residence is on the shore of a lake or river, or on the coast. Most places have a sauna, while another essential adjunct to the lakeside or seaside cottage is a boat. Between them the Finns own over 200,000 rowing boats, more than any other country in Europe, over 26,000 power boats and more than 5,000 sailing boats.

SPORT

Finns take a great interest in many kinds of sport—both as participants and observers. A survey published in the midsixties showed that over 2 million of the population belonged to some kind of athletic club. The same survey showed that the most popular sports were as follows (figures in brackets show estimated number of adherents): ball games, including ice-hockey (720,000), track and field events (375,000), ski-ing (360,000), gymnastics (190,000), orienteering (140,000), swimming (110,000), wrestling and boxing (55,000), skating (35,000), cycling (29,000).

In winter the most popular team-game is ice-hockey, and the leading clubs take part in a national league, while Finland also participates in international matches and the annual world championship matches. 'Bandy', a game similar to ice-hockey but played with a ball on a pitch the size of a football field, is another winter sport. Indoor games include volleyball and netball, while gymnastics are also very popular. Indoor tennis courts are available in many towns, but tend to be rather expensive, an hour's game costing about £1 ($2.45).

In the old days ski-ing was not so much a sport as a necessity, owing to the restrictions placed on cross-country travel by snow, and this is recognised in the Oulu *tervakilpailu* or tar-race, claimed to be the oldest ski-ing competition of its kind in the world. Similar championships are held throughout the country, the main emphasis being on cross-country rather than slalom ski-ing, using lighter and longer skis. Ski-jumping is also popular and a number of centres hold international competitions, the most important being the Salpausselkä games held in Lahti.

In summer *pesäpallo* (Finnish baseball) and football take the place of ice-hockey and ski-ing, though opportunities for international competition, particularly in the former sport, are limited. As in Britain football pools (*veikkaus*) are done winter and summer, being based on English matches in the winter and those in the Finnish league during the summer months. However, unlike the British pools it is not possible to win very large sums of money, and the majority of the profits go to improve sports facilities.

The Finns take a keen interest in international sport and since 1908 have sent a national team to the Olympic Games.

In 1912 the Finnish team came second to the USA in track and field events, while in 1924, at the Paris Olympics, Paavo Nurmi gave Finnish athletics their finest hour, winning five gold medals. In recent years Finnish Olympic successes have been more modest, but at the 1972 Games Lasse Viren, a 23-year-old policeman, won golds in the 5,000 and 10,000 metres. The previous year another Finn, Juha Väätäinen, had won these races in the European Championships in Helsinki, becoming a household name overnight and subsequently standing for parliament. He was not elected, but it is a fact that a number of Finnish politicians have in their early days won fame as sportsmen, perhaps the most notable being President Kekkonen, who was a champion high jumper during the inter-war years.

Many communes provide sports facilities for their inhabitants, while the home of Finnish sport is the Olympic Stadium in Helsinki, scene of the 1952 Olympics. There are two national sports organisations, TUL (Worker's Sports Association) and SVUL (The Finnish Gymnastics and Sports Association), and these provide facilities and instruction for their members. Gymnastic training is given in schools, which also organise ski-ing and skating competitions. Many schools have a special ski-ing day when virtually all the pupils and many of the staff ski to school, and the day is given over to ski-ing competitions of various kinds. However neither at school nor university is there as much stress on competitive sport as in Britain or the United States. Inter-school and inter-university fixtures do take place, but there is nothing of the fervour that accompanies a key rugby match at a British university, far less the excitement of an American inter-college football game. The Finns in fact tend to excel in sports that place an emphasis on individual effort rather than in team games.

One important element in Finnish sporting life is inter-Nordic competition; the annual Finnish-Swedish athletics match is followed with the closest attention. Competition is also strong in winter sports, while in recent years Finns have come to rival Swedes in rally-driving. In 1970 the World Cup Rally was won by Hannu Mikkola, while Rauno Aaltonen and Timo Mäkinen are also well known on the rally-driving circuit.

THE THEATRE

There are thirty-three professional theatres in Finland, four of which give performances in Swedish. Most Finnish theatres receive generous assistance from public funds, and the commercial theatre, as it exists in Britain and the United States, is virtually unknown. In 1971 the Ministry of Education gave £420,000 ($1,008,000) to the theatre, the majority of it going to the national or municipal theatres, though organisations like *Ylioppilasteatteri* (The Student Theatre) in Helsinki also benefited. In addition to state aid municipal theatres also get support, up to 60 or 70 per cent of their needs, from the commune which they serve. It is usual for a theatre to have several plays running at the same time, and these are performed by a resident company, the members of which have a long-term contract with the theatre. Many regular theatre-goers purchase a season ticket for their local theatre, and this helps to ensure that even an unpopular play is not a total disaster. In 1970 the theatre audience was 1,703,488, 115,542 more than in 1969.

Finnish theatres are often modern buildings, extremely well-appointed from the point of view of both actor and audience. A number have two auditoriums, while *Suomen Kansallisteatteri* (The Finnish National Theatre) in Helsinki has three, the main auditorium having seats for 912, the smaller for 311, while the 'third' auditorium provides 115 places for those who wish to see experimental or minority-interest drama. Even smaller is the *Teatteri Jurkka*, a commercial theatre in Helsinki, which has only 50 seats arranged around two sides of a large room. The largest theatre auditorium in Helsinki, and indeed in Finland, is that of the strikingly modern *Helsingin Kaupunginteatteri* (Helsinki City Theatre) with 920 seats. Including the National Opera, Helsinki has seven theatres, having 4,851 seats altogether. There are both Finnish and Swedish-speaking theatre schools in the capital, and a drama studio is attached to the University of Tampere.

The Finnish theatre season lasts from September to May, and during the summer most of the professional theatres close their doors, their place being taken by the *Kesäteatterit* (summer theatres) which put on open-air productions of old Finnish plays, musicals and similar fare. The most famous of these open-air theatres is Tampere's *Pyynikki* Theatre, a theatre-in-the-round with a difference, for the stage runs around the circumference of the 800-seat auditorium, which revolves in order that the audience can follow the action.

As might be expected, the majority of plays produced are by Finnish authors, but there is also considerable interest in the work of foreign playwrights. In the 1969–70 season there were 1,854 performances of Finnish plays, while the most popular foreign plays were English (807 performances), French (490), Russian (310) and American (122). Finland has produced no playwright of international standing to put beside the Norwegian Ibsen or the Swedish Strindberg, but nevertheless a number of Finnish writers enjoy high regard in their own country. Finnish writers have, at least in the past, tended to concentrate on domestic rather than universal themes, which has meant that their appeal is somewhat limited outside Finland. Another difficulty is that of language. Few people outside Finland understand Finnish, and though translations of Finnish works do exist the structure of Finnish is so different from the majority of other languages that even the best translations cannot catch the mood of the original.

The Finnish National Opera (*Suomen Kansallisooppera*) has its home in a charming little building in Helsinki which used to be the garrison theatre in Russian times. A number of Finnish singers have made international names for themselves, notably Kim Borg, Anita Välkki and Matti Lehtinen. In 1971 the new *Finlandiatalo* was opened, which will serve as a centre for opera, ballet and concerts, in addition to being available for conferences.

MUSIC

If Finnish authors have been isolated from the world because of the introspection of their work and the restrictions of language, there is at least one Finnish artist who has used a form that is understood the world over. Jean Sibelius is none the less very much a product of Finland, and he drew his inspiration from the *Kalevala* and other folk culture and mythology of his country, and—like many other Finnish artists—was greatly influenced by the nationalist movement at the end of the nineteenth century. In all Sibelius composed seven symphonies and numerous other works which are found in the repertoires of orchestras throughout the world. Another composer influenced by the *Kalevala* was Oskar Merikanto, who wrote an opera *The Maid of Pohjola* in 1899, while Erkki Melartin's opera *Aino* derives from the same source. In addition Melartin has written seven symphonies. The best-known living composers in Finland are probably Einojuhani Rautavaara and Tauno Marttinen, both of whom have written operas and orchestral music.

Helsinki has three symphony orchestras, including that of the National Opera, and a chamber orchestra, while there are also orchestras in the leading provincial centres. Singing is popular and many churches, schools, universities and other organisations have choirs which give concerts in their home towns and also further afield. There are also a number of folk-song and dance clubs which keep alive some of the Finnish traditional music. As with the theatre the regular music season extends from September to May, but during the summer months there are a number of festivals. The largest and most important of these is the Helsinki festival, held in June, while others are held in Turku, Savonlinna, Vaasa and other towns. For those who do not get a chance to visit concerts the radio broadcasts frequent music programmes. Over 50 per cent of the output of Finnish radio is music, some 33 per cent being classical.

Light music and pop music also have a large following, and

in addition to the international pop-stars the Finns have their home-produced versions, including Irwin Goodman—whose choice of stage-name has caused the author a certain amount of embarrassment—Danny and Tapani Kansa, in addition to groups of varying skill and enthusiasm. In spite of their loyalty to their domestic idols, however, the appeal of British and American groups and singers is extremely strong, and international pop-stars have many devoted followers among the Finnish younger generation. Since 1966 a jazz festival has been held in the west coast town of Pori, while Finland's best-known pop festival is 'Ruisrock', which takes place just outside Turku.

THE CINEMA

In 1957, the year before television was introduced in Finland, there were 613 cinemas in the country, and the total audience for the year was 32 million; in 1970 there were 327 cinemas, and an audience of 11·7 million.

The majority of films shown in Finland are imported; in 1970 221 films had first nights, 13 of which were Finnish, 76 American, 21 French, 17 English and 16 Italian, while others screened included films from the USSR, Sweden and Czechoslovakia. Films are almost invariably shown in the original language, with both Swedish and Finnish subtitles.

During the sixties a total of 114 full-length films were made in Finland, the peak year being 1962 when 22 were produced, the slackest 1967 when the total was 3. As yet Finnish films have not been able to establish a distinctive national identity and tend, as far as technique is concerned, to borrow much from foreign countries without having much to contribute in exchange. To a certain extent the Finnish film industry has been overshadowed by that of Sweden, and it also suffers from the fact that in many countries a 'Scandinavian film' means a sex film. For example an inoffensive story about four young people camping on an island in central Finland, entitled 'Käpy selän alla' (literally 'Fircones under the back') was renamed 'Skin' for English audiences, and billed in at least one cinema as 'The Finish [*sic*] film they dared not show in Sweden'.

In 1970 the Tampere International Short Film Festival was held for the first time, and in 1971 222 films from 34 different countries were shown.

RADIO AND TELEVISION

Radio broadcasting in Finland dates from 1926, when state-owned radio stations started to put out programmes supplied by private companies. In 1934, however, *Oy Yleisradio Ab* (The Finnish Broadcasting Company) was established as a joint-stock company, nine-tenths of the shares of which were owned by the government. Television transmissions were pioneered in 1955 by the Finnish Radio Engineers' Association, but when public broadcasts started in 1958 they were under the control of Yleisradio, which in practice has a monopoly of radio and television broadcasting in Finland. However Yleisradio hires out television time to Oy Mainos-TV-Reklam Ab, a commercial company owned by leading advertising interests, and in 1970 this company transmitted 722 hours of programmes, compared with YTV's 2,750 hours. Finland has two television channels, and MTV rents time on both, which means that commercial and non-commercial programmes can be seen one after the other.

Television licences, which cost £8.37 ($20.5), account for 47·3 per cent of the income of Yleisradio, while a further 26·4 per cent comes from radio licences, costing £2.80 ($6.86). Advertising is the third main source, accounting for some 22 per cent of the company's income.

In 1969 there were 1,015,308 television sets in Finland (about 1,000 of which were colour sets), that is 216 for every 1,000 inhabitants. The figure for the United Kingdom in 1969 was 15,632, 978 or 286 sets for every 1,000, and for the United States about 82,200,000, 409 sets per 1,000. In the same year 371 Finns out of every 1,000 had a radio, compared with 316 per 1,000 in Britain and 1,148 per 1,000 for the USA.

The radio network covers the whole country, about 98 per cent of the population being within reach of radio transmissions, though only about 75 per cent are in fact reached; for television the figures are 76 per cent and 65 per cent respectively. The second television channel is at present received by 50 per cent of the population, concentrated in the south, but its coverage is gradually being extended northwards. There are three radio networks, two of which broadcast in Finnish and are on the air for an average of 213 hours a week, while the Swedish network broadcasts for 71 hours a week. It is estimated that during 1970 Yleisradio broadcast more than 15,420 hours. The radio networks transmit from 6 am to midnight, though the two television channels tend to concentrate their programmes, apart from education and sport, in the evenings. There are about 70 hours of television each week, about 35 per cent of which consists of imported programmes, usually British or American.

External broadcasting in Finnish began during the 1940s and in 1967 an English language service was also started. 'Hear Finland', which is financed jointly by Yleisradio and the Ministry of Foreign Affairs, broadcasts for about seven hours each week.

BOOKS

During 1970 3,520 books were published in Finland. A total of 785 were translated from other languages, 415 of them from English. Finnish books tend to be rather expensive, however, since the market is virtually confined to the 4·6 million Finns living in Finland (English and American publishers have a theoretical market of 300 million, not counting those who speak English as a second language). Foreign books imported into Finland are also very expensive.

The Finns are well served by their public libraries, about 30 million books being borrowed from the 3,015 libraries run by the local authorities each year. There are also a number of specialist libraries, while the university libraries, with nearly 4 million volumes on their shelves, are open to the general public in addition to members of the university, a highly commendable way of ensuring that knowledge is freely available to all. The finest library in the country is undoubtedly that belonging to the University of Helsinki, which receives a copy of each book published in Finland, and which also has an extensive collection of Scandinavian and Russian books, the latter being one of the best outside the Soviet Union.

For reasons mentioned earlier Finnish writers are not all that well known abroad, even though some Finnish books have been widely translated; the works of F. E. Sillanpää (who was awarded the Nobel Prize for Literature in 1939), for example, have been translated into twenty-four languages. Until the Reformation, written Finnish was but poorly developed, and even after that time most educated Finns wrote and spoke Swedish. Thus it is not until the nineteenth century that there is any real evidence of a genuine Finnish literature. Nevertheless there was an extremely strong oral tradition, and it is these folk stories that Elias Lönnrot used as the basis of the *Kalevala*. It is now generally agreed that Lönnrot himself added to and edited the material he collected in order to make the epic poem a harmonious whole, though this does nothing to detract from its importance both in the history of Finnish nationalism and Finnish literature. For many Finns of the nineteenth century the ancient folk-lays provided the cultural ancestry they were looking for, while since that time the epic has inspired composers, artists and writers. Other great names of Finnish literature are the Swedish-Finnish poet Johan Runeberg—the first stanzas of whose best-known work *Tales of Ensign Ståhl* became the Finnish national anthem, *Maamme* (Our Land)—and Alexis Kivi, who provided the Finns with a mirror for their national character in his novel *Seitsemän Veljestä* (Seven Brothers).

Recent Finnish writers include Mika Waltari, best-known abroad for his historical romances, and Väinö Linna, whose *Tuntematon Sotilas* (The Unknown Soldier), set in the Continuation War, caused a sensation when it was first published in 1954.

Contemporary authors such as Eila Pennanen, Pentti Saari-
koski, Hannu Salama and Paavo Rintala have a large following
in Finland but tend to be little known outside their own
country, as with a few exceptions their work is not available in
translation. Most of the classics of world literature can be read
in Finnish, while a large number of modern works from many
countries have also been translated.

NEWSPAPERS AND MAGAZINES

While Finland does not have a national press centred on the
capital as in Britain, the country is not large enough to have as
much diversity as there is in the United States. Virtually every
town of any size in Finland publishes a morning paper, but the
leading Helsinki newspapers can also be bought in most parts
of the country on the same day as they are published. In all
there are 89 papers appearing three or more times a week, and
a further 122 which come out once a week; 20 of the former and
7 of the latter are in Swedish. Daily sales of papers in Finland
are about 40 for every 100 people, compared with 48 per 100
for Britain and 32 per 100 for the USA.

Finland's largest paper is *Helsingin Sanomat,* which has a circulation of 271,798 (1970), and would be classified as a
'quality' in British terms. Unlike many Finnish papers *Helsingin
Sanomat* is not owned by a political party and tends to follow an
independent if rather conservative line. Both Tampere and
Turku have papers with circulations over the 100,000 mark.
Aamulehti (109,000) is owned by the National Coalition Party
and published in Tampere, while Turku's daily *Turun Sanomat*
(107,000) is non-party. The National Coalition Party also own
Uusi Suomi (84,000), which is published in Helsinki, and a
number of provincial papers. As in many other countries the
voice of the Left tends to be somewhat muted when it comes to
newspapers; the communist paper *Kansan Uutiset* had a circulation of 43,878 in 1970 (which nevertheless compares favourably

with the British *Morning Star*, 49,493 in the same year), while *Suomen Sosiaalidemokraatti*, controlled by the Social Democratic Party, went to 38,457 homes. The largest Swedish-language newspaper, *Hufvudstadsbladet*, is independent, but naturally takes a close interest in matters concerning the Swedish-Finns; it has a circulation of about 66,000. Finland's first newspaper was in Swedish and was started in 1771, to be followed five years later by the first Finnish-language paper, *Suomenkieliset Tieto Sanomat*.

The state pays grants to some Finnish newspapers each year; in 1971, for example, nearly £750,000 ($1.8 million) was paid out to fifty newspapers to help with their transport and distribution costs. The papers that benefited most were published by the Centre, Social Democratic and Communist Parties, and this has led to criticism in some quarters that the state is subsidising political parties. But it seems clear that without such support a number of papers would find it difficult to continue, and supporters of the subsidy scheme argue that in a free society it is important that all points of view should be heard.

In addition to newspapers there are over 1,500 periodicals catering for all tastes and published in a number of languages, though those in Finnish and Swedish naturally predominate.

ART GALLERIES AND MUSEUMS

Finland's great pride in its past is reflected in its large number of museums. The impressive National Museum in Helsinki traces the history of Finland from earliest times to the present day, while other museums in the capital include the Helsinki City Museum, the Zoological Museum, the Railway Museum and the Atheneum Art Gallery, which, in addition to housing the national art collection, also arranges exhibitions. One of the most interesting sights in Helsinki is Seurasaari, where houses and other buildings from all over Finland have been re-erected on an island a few miles from the city centre.

Turku has its own open-air museum in the form of the *Käsityö-läismuseo* (Handicraft Museum), housed in wooden buildings on the side of one of the city's seven hills. Unlike Seurasaari, however, most of the houses in the Turku museum were built where they stand today, for the area is part of the old town that survived the disastrous fire of 1827. Uusikaupunki on the west coast has a collection of windmills, while at Mariehamn in Åland is an impressive maritime museum containing relics from the last days of sail. Other places in the country have their local museums, showing how the previous inhabitants of the area carried on their everyday life, for the stress in most Finnish collections is on things that directly concern their country and the way in which the people used to live.

Albert Edelfelt and Akseli Gallen-Kallela are probably the best-known Finnish painters. Edelfelt (1854–1905) was greatly influenced by the French Naturalists, bringing their techniques to Finland and using them in his realistic and sympathetic paintings of Finnish country people. Gallen-Kallela (1865–1931) was one of the leading figures of the National Romantic Movement. Like many other Finnish artists he was greatly influenced by the *Kalevala*, and some of his best-known pictures illustrate scenes from the national epic.

In recent years Finnish sculpture has been experiencing a renaissance, stimulated to some extent by the development of new architectural schemes in which sculpture is considered to be an integral part, and also by the willingness of public and private institutions to commission new works. The leading figure of this renaissance is undoubtedly Väinö Aaltonen (1898–1966). In addition to statues and busts of his famous countrymen, such as Paavo Nurmi, Alexis Kivi, K. J. Ståhlberg and Jean Sibelius, Aaltonen produced many striking sculptures of human figures and more abstract designs in granite—perhaps his most characteristic material—marble and bronze. Other prominent sculptors include Tapio Wirkkala, who is particularly interested in the possibilities offered by laminated wood and glass, Aimo Tukiainen, whose best-known work is the equestrian statue of Mannerheim in Helsinki, and Eila Hiltunen, the sculptress who was responsible for the impressive Sibelius monument, completed in 1967.

HOLIDAYS

As we have seen, for many Finns the ideal holiday is to retire into the depths of the country and spend a few days as far away as possible from other people. For most Finns the essential ingredients of a good holiday place are water and sun, and good weather will bring out crowds of people hurrying to the local bathing beach on the coast or the shore of lake or river. Camping and caravanning, either in Finland or abroad, are also becoming increasingly popular. In fact, in common with people from other countries, the Finns are travelling away from their own country for holidays to an ever-increasing extent. In 1970 about one in every seventeen Finns, 267,562 of them, went abroad (abroad in this context meaning out of the Nordic passport area). The most popular months for foreign travel are May to August inclusive, nearly half those who go abroad doing so during these four months. Winter package tours have become very popular in recent years, and a considerable number of Finns travel to Spain or the South of France between December and March, 'to get away from the Finnish winter for a few days'. A popular Easter destination is the Soviet Union, and every year between 5,000 and 6,000 Finns travel to Leningrad and other Russian cities by bus or train. Lapland is also an Easter attraction, especially for ski-ing enthusiasts; in 1972, for example, more than 20,000 tourists from southern Finland spent their Easter on the Lapland fells.

Part of the UKK package (see p 73) was to extend the length of the annual leave to four weeks. In addition to this annual holiday, the Finns observe the following public holidays: 1 January; Good Friday; Easter Monday; 1 May (*Vappu*); Midsummer (*Juhannus*, on the nearest Saturday to 24 June); All Saints' Day; Independence Day (6 December); Christmas

Day and Boxing Day (*tapaninpäivä*). Many of these festivals actually begin the day before, *aatto*, which often means that shops, banks and other places close at midday, a fact that should be borne in mind by foreigners, unless they want to run the risk of starving over a holiday period.

8

The Lapps and Lapland

ENGLISH usage implies that the Lapps are the nationals of Lapland just as the Finns are nationals of Finland. However the Lapps, although a distinct people, have never had their own state, and at the present time are citizens of Norway, Sweden, Finland or the USSR. The area referred to as 'Lapland' is indefinite, and is perhaps best described as the region where the Lapps live and where the Lappish language is spoken (though of course other people live, and other languages are spoken, in this area). According to this rough definition, Lapland extends from the Arctic Ocean in the north to Lake Femund, about 180 miles from Oslo, in the south. In the west Lapps can be found on the Atlantic coast of Norway, and in the east in the Kola peninsula and on the shores of the White Sea.

It is estimated that there are 34–35,000 Lapps in the world today, but for reasons explained later it is virtually impossible to arrive at an accurate figure. The greater part of the present-day Lapp population live in Norway, mainly in the provinces of Troms, Nordland and Finnmark (which means 'borderland of the Lapps' in Norwegian). Sweden's Lapps number about 10,000 and are found in the western areas of Jämtland, Västerbotten and Norrbotten, while the 2,500 to 3,000 Lapps in Finland are concentrated in the northernmost parishes of the vast province of Lappi (Lappland in Swedish). There are thought to be between 1,500 and 2,000 Lapps living in the Soviet Union, the majority of whom are to be found in the Kola peninsula.

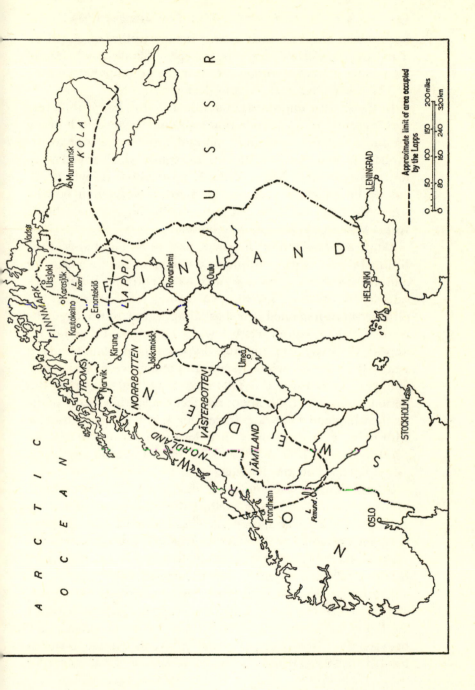

Lapps seem to prefer their own company to that of outsiders. They are the shortest people in Europe—the average height of men is 5ft 2½in and of women 4ft 10¼in. Most Lapps have brown or black hair and darkish complexions.

In the southernmost areas inhabited by the Lapps the great coniferous forests in earlier times provided extensive hunting grounds. Further north the pine and spruce give way to the dwarf trees and bushes of the tundra region, which stretches up to the Arctic coast. Much of the Lapp territory is high, particularly in Finnmark and on the Swedish-Norwegian border, where the land rises to over 6,000 feet, the highest point being Kebnekajse, 6,960 feet, in Norrbotten.

While the Lapland of the travel posters is 'The Land of the Midnight Sun', with continuous daylight in the far north for almost three months, there is of course a correspondingly dark side to the picture. During November, long after the last reindeer-horn-festooned car has disappeared south over the Arctic Circle, the sun sinks below the horizon and does not reappear for some two months. Lapland is predominantly a winter land, for the winter begins in the first week of October, and lasts until early the following May. For much of this period the snow cover is about two feet thick, while many of the smaller Lapland lakes are frozen for seven or eight months, with only the map to show their location. Mean winter temperatures range from 8° F to 0° F, and can easily fall below − 14° F, especially on the fells.

Spring comes in the middle of May, the rise in temperature to between 32° F and 60° F melting the snow cover, almost invariably causing widespread flooding. Summer lasts in some areas for up to eighty days and during this time temperatures vary considerably, with hot sunny weather in the mid-70s F being quickly followed by cold spells and even frosts, which have a disastrous effect on cultivation. Autumn comes in a brief, glorious blaze of colour, and temperatures drop to between 40° F and 32° F. In spite of the fact that most of Lapland lies between the latitudes of 71° N and 66° N, the climate is not as harsh as in other areas as far north, in Alaska and Canada, for example. This is largely due to the modifying influence of the Gulf Stream and to the absence of cold Arctic currents. Temperatures in Lapland are also affected by the direction of the winds; those from the south or Atlantic have a favourable effect, but should the wind direction veer to north or east the temperature falls rapidly. Because of the short growing season crops such as wheat cannot be grown north of the Arctic Circle. However, the 100 to 120-day growing season has proved sufficient for barley, oats and potatoes, which can be sown in the region of the Arctic Circle in May and be harvested in August or September.

HISTORY OF THE LAPPS

The origin of the Lapps is something of a mystery. One school of thought believes that they were the aboriginal population of Finland and northern Scandinavia, while others give them, like the Finns, an Asiatic homeland from which the Lapps migrated some time before the Finns. The second argument is largely based on the fact that both the Finnish and Lappish tongues belong to the Finno-Ugrian family, but supporters of the first theory suggest that the Lapps may have originally spoken an entirely different language which was then replaced or modified by Finnish. 'No one has ever heard that the Lapps came to this land from any other place. From the very earliest times they have been up here in Lappland; and when, in the beginning, the Lapps lived by the sea coast, there wasn't a single other person living here,' claims the Lapp writer Joahn Turi. If we take Turi at his word it seems that the Lapps were living in Lapland some 8,000 years ago, for stone implements that old have been found on the coast of Finnmark. Turi is a far from scientific source, as he relied on the stories and legends of his people for much of his information, but some experts do believe it possible that the Lapps lived in the area as long ago as that. In addition to the Finnmark finds, a number of artefacts have been discovered in different places in Sweden and Finland that date back 4,000 years, as well as rock drawings thought to be 3,000 years old. While it cannot be proved conclusively that any of the finds are the work of Lapps, as yet there is no evidence of any pre-Lapp race who might have been responsible.

As we have seen, opinions differ as to whether Tacitus's wild 'Fenni' were Finns, Lapps or the products of his imagination stimulated by second-hand accounts of northern tribes. There is, however, evidence that the Lapps were living in Scandinavia at the time, and as far south as the Gulf of Finland. It is generally believed that as the Finns began to penetrate inland, along the shores of the rivers and lakes, the Lapps either moved to hunting grounds further north or were assimilated by the Finns. It has also been suggested that even at this stage in their history the life of the Lapps was bound up with the reindeer, and that as the wild reindeer moved northwards the Lapps followed in their tracks. It is not known for certain when the Lapps became reindeer-herders, but in a report made by the Norwegian chieftain Ottar to King Alfred of Wessex in 892 the Lapps are referred to as hunters who also keep reindeer. Ottar himself claimed to have a herd of 600 of the animals.

The Lapps' withdrawal northwards seems to have been a gradual process, and a map produced by Dr T. Itkonen, one of the leading authorities on the Lapps, shows that at the beginning of the thirteenth century they could be found throughout Finland with the exception of the south and south-west coastal regions. By the sixteenth century they were concentrated in the eastern and northern areas of the country, but it was not until the last century that those in Finland had moved north of the Arctic Circle. It is not clear to what extent the Finns and the Lapps inter-married during the course of history, but it is generally thought that many Finns, especially those from the north and east of the country, have a considerable amount of Lapp blood in their veins.

Whereas in Finland the Lapps moved north in the face of Finnish colonisation, in Sweden and Norway many Lapps came south, particularly when the Swedes left Vilhelmina and

Umeå Lappmarks as the climate deteriorated. By the end of the Middle Ages they were living as far south as Namdel and Jämtland. In the eighteenth century the Lapps in Norway were reported south of Trondheim, while in 1889 they were granted pasture on both sides of the northern part of Lake Femund, on the basis of 'time-honoured right'.

Although there is a wealth of legends and stories about early Lapp life, little is known about the way in which Lapp society was organised. There appears to have been no centralised administration and the majority of the Lapps seem to have lived in family or tribal groups, supporting themselves by hunting and fishing organised on a co-operative basis. The term *siida* or Lapp village is used by Reindeer Lapps to describe a group who migrate together, but it has been suggested that the *siida* was originally the co-operative unit of the hunting and fishing culture. In addition to hunting for their own needs the Lapps bartered beaver, reindeer and bear skins with their Swedish, Finnish and Novgorodian neighbours, receiving weapons, tools and ornaments in exchange. During the Middle Ages trade with Lapps was dominated by the Finnish *pirkkalaiset* or *bircals* who had been granted a trading monopoly by the Swedish crown, and these men were also responsible for collecting taxes from the Lapps. The power of the *bircals* was brought to an end by Gustavus Vasa, who withdrew their privileges and ordered the Lapps to pay their taxes direct to the crown. Gustavus Vasa also announced that the wilderness lands belonged 'to God, to us and to the Swedish crown', a claim that was re-affirmed by Charles XI in 1683, when he stated that the wilds were the personal property of the crown. These measures limited the rights of the Lapps, as they had no title to their hunting grounds apart from the fact that their ancestors had hunted over them for generations.

The ownership of the lands of the north is unclear during much of the Middle Ages. In 1323 the Swedes and Novgorodians had signed a frontier treaty, but the line of the border was not clearly defined in the wild forest lands, causing both sides to claim certain areas. Nor were Sweden and Novgorod the only claimants, for at the beginning of the fourteenth century the Norwegians established a castle and taxation office at Vardö, in order to collect taxes from the Lapps. The Swedes and Novgorodians also sent their tax-collectors out into the forests, which meant that sometimes the unfortunate Lapps were expected to pay taxes to three masters. If the tax-collector was particularly zealous he might also impose a fine if he thought that taxes had been paid to his competitors. The frontier established between Sweden and the Duchy of Moscovy in 1595 failed to solve the problem, as shortly after the agreement was made Charles IX claimed the whole of Lapland, as far as the Arctic Ocean and the White Sea, for Sweden, styling himself 'King of the Lapps'. Christian IV, King of Denmark-Norway, took exception to the title and its implications, and in 1613 Charles's successor, Gustavus Adolphus, was forced to renounce it and accept Danish control of the Arctic coast.

Although the early Lapps tended to concentrate on hunting and fishing, their way of life gradually changed, and from the sixteenth or seventeenth centuries onwards the emergence of distinctive occupational groups can be seen. As the great herds of wild reindeer decreased in size, some of the Lapp population turned from being hunters and became herders of reindeer. It is among these Lapps that the classic pattern of Lapp reindeer nomadism was established. For these Reindeer or Mountain Lapps hunting became a subsidiary activity, their main occupation being the tending of the reindeer herds, moving with them from the mountains to the coastal areas according to the time of year. In the forest regions, particularly those of north Sweden-Finland, hunting remained important and these Lapps only domesticated a few reindeer, to be used as beasts of burden, milch animals or decoys for trapping wild reindeer. The basis of the Forest Lapps' economy was hunting and trapping, supplemented by freshwater fishing, though in more recent times farming has become of increasing importance in this group. The Coast Lapps also carried on the hunting tradition, but their main means of livelihood was fishing. Another group to whom fishing was important were the River Lapps, but in their case they caught freshwater fish from lakes and rivers. Both the Forest Lapps and the Coast Lapps were semi-nomadic, in that they moved from place to place in pursuit of game or fish.

Semi-nomadism based on reindeer herding was also found among the Skolt and Kola Lapps. The characteristic that chiefly distinguishes these groups from their relatives in Norway, Sweden and Finland is that they have been exposed to Russian influence for centuries, and therefore tend to be eastern in religion and culture. Whereas the western Lapps belong to the Lutheran tradition, the Skolt and Kola Lapps are members of the Orthodox Church.

The changes in the Lapp way of life occurred gradually, but nevertheless from the sixteenth century onwards a Lapp culture was developing that was in many ways quite distinct from that of the Middle Ages and earlier. To a certain extent this was due to changes such as the decline of the wild reindeer and other animals, but other factors which must be taken into account are the contraction of the hunting grounds and the growth of outside influences as settlers moved in from the south.

We have already seen that as the Lapps moved northwards settlers followed them, and the same pattern has continued right up to the present day. Between 1630 and 1758, when the first Finns settled at Inari, for example, the Finns colonised the whole of the Kemi Lappmark, establishing their farms in the areas where the Lapps had previously hunted wild reindeer, beaver and other animals. In 1670 an edict was published permitting the Finns and the Lapps to live side by side, provided they pursued different occupations. This was to prove difficult for the Lapps, as reindeer-herding and hunting do not co-exist easily with farming; the Finns accused them of allowing reindeer to damage their crops, while for their part the Lapps resented the incursion of the Finns into land they regarded as their own. Although at first the Lapps retained some privileges these were gradually whittled away. In 1747, for instance, the 'beaver right', which gave the Lapps the exclusive right to trap beaver, was abolished, allowing the Finns to compete on equal terms.

It was through measures such as this that the old hunting culture of the Kemi Lappmark disappeared during the eighteenth century, to be replaced by the culture of the settlers.

A similar pattern could be seen in other parts of the north. During the reign of Queen Christina (1632–44) precious metals were discovered in Norrbotten, and the Lapps and their reindeer were pressed into service to transport the ore from the mines to the coast. On the credit side, in 1751 a frontier treaty was signed between Sweden and Norway-Denmark, which among other things gave the Lapps the right to cross the Swedish-Norwegian border in search of water and pasture for their animals. About the same time the boundaries of the 'lappmarks' were fixed in Sweden, protecting the rights of the Lapps to the fishing waters and hunting grounds they had been accustomed to use. But infringements still took place, and in 1830 the Lapps appealed to the king; as a result land was granted them for pasture. During the first half of the nineteenth century the reindeer-herders passed freely over the borders of Norway and what was, after 1809, the Grand Duchy of Finland. In 1851, however, the tsar prohibited the Norwegian Lapps from crossing the border, and in 1889 the frontier between Sweden and Finland was also closed.

The introduction of Christianity from the seventeenth century onwards also had an effect on the pattern of Lapp life. The missionaries regarded the nature religion of the Lapps with horror and took strong action to stamp it out, destroying as they did so the drums used in religious rituals and other important elements of the ancient Lapp culture. The teaching of one of the most important of these missionaries, Lars Levi Laestadius, who was active at the beginning of the nineteenth century, still has an important influence among the Lapp community today.

The incursion of settlers into Lapp areas continued during the nineteenth century and into the twentieth, bringing some benefits but also many problems for the Lapp way of life. The full implications of these, and the general position of the Lapps today are dealt with in the next chapter.

9

How the Lapps Live and Work

THE age-old problem for the Lapp people has been to avoid being swallowed up by ever-encroaching majority populations. Historically the Lapps have tended to live in areas where the Finnish, Norwegian or Swedish population was either small or non-existent. When settlers arrived and a culture conflict arose, the Lapps either moved or were absorbed. Today, however, there is nowhere left for the Lapps to move to, and consequently the threat of absorption has become much greater. The development of communications, the discovery of raw materials, the establishment of new hydro-electric schemes and industries in the Lapp areas have all contributed to this situation, as has compulsory education in schools which do not always provide education in the Lappish language. Some Lapps and those interested in their problems feel that Lapp culture and language must be preserved, but many of the Lapp population are apparently indifferent, while others seem positively to welcome absorption, as they believe that being a Lapp and speaking Lappish restricts their chances—and their children's chances—of advancement.

As pointed out earlier, estimates which put the number of Lapps at between 34,000 and 35,000 must be accepted with a certain reserve, as there is no generally accepted definition of a Lapp. The obvious criterion might appear to be language, as was proposed by the Finnish Commission on Lapp Affairs in 1951, but even this is not straightforward. Studies made in Finland and Sweden have shown that each year a number of Lappish-speakers change to the language of the majority population. One of the commonest reasons for this seems to be marriage: when a Lapp marries a non-Lapp, he or she almost invariably adopts the language of the spouse, largely because, while Lapps tend to be bi- or even trilingual, the members of the majority populations rarely speak Lappish. There are also instances of marriages where both partners originally spoke Lappish but have changed to Finnish or Swedish, perhaps to assist their children's education. Again, if a Lapp takes a job which requires the use of the majority language, the language used at work may gradually become the home-language too. As education, particularly of an advanced or specialised nature, is frequently not available in Lappish, a Lapp wishing to study in advanced fields may neglect his own language because he feels it only has a limited value for him. Factors such as these mean that a considerable number of people of Lapp descent do not speak Lappish. This state of affairs was recognised by the proposal of the Nordic Lapp Council that a Lapp should be defined as a person whose parents, or father's or mother's parents, speak or have spoken Lappish as their home language.

HOW THE LAPPS WORK

Although certain features of the occupational division which took place during the sixteenth and seventeenth centuries can still be seen, in many cases the distinctions have become blurred. The shortage of game and improved methods of fishing have driven many Forest and Coast Lapps away from their old means of livelihood, while a considerable number of Reindeer Lapps too have given up their traditional way of life. Today Lapps are found in a wide variety of jobs, working on the land, in mining, as truck-drivers and labourers, while both men and women can be found in the service industries.

It has been suggested by some authorities that the survival of the Lapp culture depends on the reindeer, but today only about 17 per cent of the Lapps rely on reindeer as their main source of income: in Finland about 37 per cent, in Sweden 20 per cent and in Norway a mere 8 per cent of the Lapp population are engaged in full-time reindeer-breeding. At the end of the 1960s there were probably about 600,000 reindeer in the Nordic countries—about 180,000 in Finland, 170,000 in Norway and some 250,000 in Sweden. There are thought to be about 2 million reindeer in the Soviet Union, not all of these in Lapp areas. In Finland, Finns as well as Lapps are permitted to keep reindeer, and only about a quarter of the country's stock is in Lapp hands. The reindeer-breeding area—which extends south of the province of Lappi, into that of Oulu—is divided into organisations of reindeer herders—*paliskunnat*—each one with a chairman elected from among its members. The central body of these co-operative associations is *Paliskuntain Yhdistys* (the Central Association of Reindeer Breeders). In Sweden, reindeer-herding is restricted to Swedes of Lapp descent, who are members of a Lapp village and who are holders of the 'Lapp right', that is the right to breed reindeer. The 'Lapp right' gives its holders privileges regarding land use, fishing and hunting in connection with his main occupation. Should a Lapp leave the Lapp village or buy land to set up as a farmer, he loses the 'Lapp right' and is not able to regain it, even if he should prove unsuccessful as a farmer. The Norwegian counterpart of the Swedish Reindeer Lapp is the Nomad Lapp, who like his Swedish cousin has certain privileges in reindeer-breeding areas. In both Sweden and Norway non-Lapps may only keep reindeer as a subsidiary source of income.

During the summer months the reindeer are permitted to range over the pastures of the high land of northern Norway, Sweden and Finland, and then, during September and October, they are rounded up into corrals to be sorted and counted. The autumn round-up is one of the great events of the Lapp year, for it gives the reindeer-herders and their families a chance to meet, exchange gossip and news and generally enjoy themselves in the company of their fellows. Although to the eye of the layman one reindeer looks much like another, the owner is able to distinguish his beasts by the registered ear-marks.

Following the autumn sorting the animals are moved to

sheltered winter pasture on low ground. The reindeer's basic food during the coldest part of the year is lichen, which is often buried beneath thick snow. Their spade-shaped hooves are particularly well-adapted for digging in soft snow, and they can get at lichen two feet or more beneath the surface. Should the snow become too thick or freeze hard, however, grazing may become difficult, and the herdsman must check regularly to ensure that his herd is getting sufficient food. In the spring, while the snow is still on the ground, a move is made to pastures on the slopes of the fells, and it is here, towards the end of May, that the calves are born. For about a month the herds graze on the side of the uplands, while the young animals build up their strength. About midsummer the need for fresh grass, and the attentions of the mosquitoes, drive the reindeer further up the fells to the abundant pastures of the high land, where they remain until brought down for the autumn sorting once again.

In earlier times the reindeer provided the Lapp with many necessities of life, meat, milk, cheese, clothes and footwear, virtually every part of the animal being utilised, while before it was slaughtered it led a useful life as a draught or pack animal. Nowadays, however, the reindeer is kept mainly for its meat, milking has virtually ceased, and the Lapp of the twentieth century is far more likely to travel by 'sno-mobile' than the traditional boat-shaped Lapp sledge. The great migrations when whole communities moved with the herds also belong to the past, for even among the Lapps who practise reindeer-husbandry there is an increasing tendency for women, children and the older men to stay in one place, while the herds are supervised by young men living on the edge of the summer pasture. The famous conical tent, resembling an Indian tepee, constructed of poles and thick woollen blankets is rarely found nowadays, most Lapps living in dwellings hardly distinguishable from those of the majority population, though their conditions may be more overcrowded.

Although the number of people dependent on reindeer-breeding has declined—it is estimated that in 1900 4,000 Lapps in Sweden made a living from reindeer husbandry compared with half that number today—the number of animals has remained fairly constant. But whereas earlier in the century in a natural economy a family could support itself on a herd of about 200 reindeer, today's money economy requires over 400. Recently attempts have been made to improve the methods of reindeer husbandry, and it has been widely recognised that more research is required to increase the output of reindeer meat. The number of reindeer slaughtered each year varies according to the market conditions, but in Finland the annual kill is usually about 60,000 animals, worth about £1.4 million ($3.5 million). After the autumn 1971 round-up the price for reindeer carcases in Finland was about 30p (72 cents) per pound. Most of the reindeer sold by the *paliskunnat* after the round-up are bought by three large companies; in 1970 they took about 700 tons of reindeer meat between them. Although reindeer meat appears on the menus of a number of restaurants in the Nordic countries, its price means that it is not common on private tables. There is some export trade, but many potential customers seem to be discouraged by the fact that reindeer are frequently butchered outside properly equipped slaughterhouses. As for live animals, reindeer have been sent to a number of countries, including Britain, Chile and Greenland.

The Forest Lapps of Finland and Sweden were originally hunters and fishers, their most important quarry being the wild reindeer, while the River Lapps' main source of livelihood was fish, especially salmon. With the decline of game and fish, large numbers of both groups have become farmers. Although the Forest Lapps kept small numbers of reindeer for domestic purposes it was not until the supplies of wild animals began to run low that they turned to reindeer-herding on a large scale. In the past the herding methods of the Mountain Lapps and the Forest Lapps have differed, those of the latter being more intensive, but with time many of the differences have disappeared.

For the Coast Lapps (or 'Sea Finns') the reindeer was merely a beast of burden. Far more important to their way of life were the seal, walrus and whale. The Coast Lapps, found on the coast of Norway in the provinces of Finnmark, Troms and

K

Nordland (those living in the last two areas being descended from Swedish Mountain Lapps), led a semi-nomadic existence, living at the head of the fiord during the winter and moving down to the mouth as the ice melted in the spring. In earlier times, the migratory cycle was continued into the autumn, when they moved their hunting grounds from the sea to the fells inland, but since the early years of this century hunting has become more restricted, and now the Coast Lapps' land activities are centred on farming. Fishing is still practised, but improved techniques and the use of larger boats means that, although larger catches can be made, there is employment for fewer men.

During the war the Skolt Lapps living in Finland were evacuated from the Petsamo region to Ostrobothnia. When their former homes were ceded to the Soviet Union following the Continuation War, they were provided with houses built on state land in the Inari area, where the majority of them remain. In spite of the fact that in 1955 the Finnish state established a special foundation to assist the Skolt Lapps, their living conditions have remained poor and there is an urgent need for more land suitable for cultivation and more livestock. In many ways the Skolts are a minority within a minority, as most of them belong to the Orthodox Church, while their language, customs and clothing all differ from those of the western Lapps. There are about 600 Skolt Lapps in Finland and a further 500 or so who still live in the Soviet Union.

The Kola peninsula differs from the other parts of Lapland in that about 90 cer cent of its population live in urban areas, the largest city being Murmansk, which has over 220,000 inhabitants. More than 500,000 people live in the Murmansk administrative district (which is virtually co-terminal with the peninsula) about 2,000 of whom are Lapps. As in other areas the Russian Lapps today are engaged in a variety of occupations, including reindeer-herding, forestry and farming.

LANGUAGE

It is generally agreed that Finnish and Lappish belong to the same language group, but this does not mean that they are mutually intelligible. Indeed Lappish itself is split into a number of dialects, and Lapps from different areas may find it impossible to communicate unless they use a third language such as Finnish or Swedish. Mountain or Northern Lappish is the most widespread of the Lapp dialects, probably being used by about four-fifths of all Lappish speakers. In Finland, for example, it is the tongue of 66 per cent of the Lappish-speaking population while 18 per cent speak Inari Lappish and 16 per cent speak Skolt Lappish. In Norway Mountain Lappish is spoken in the Finnmark area, and it is also widely used in the northernmost Swedish province. Norrland. Further south in both Norway and Sweden the Lule, Pite, Ume and Southern Lappish dialects can be found. The Skolt Lapps in Finland and the Soviet Union speak the Skolt form of the language, while their neighbours in the Kola peninsula speak Kildin and Ter Lappish.

As might be expected, the Lapp vocabulary has many words for snow, frost, water and other natural phenomena, but few for abstract ideas and modern technological developments. There are, for example, several hundred words connected with snow, which describe its depth, consistency, the length of time it has been on the ground and so on. There are also a large number of terms associated with the reindeer; one Swedish authority, Dr Israel Ruong, estimates that about a quarter of the words in the Lapp vocabulary refer to the reindeer or reindeer-breeding. The word for reindeer herd, *ællo*, means significantly 'what one lives on', while the term used to describe a male reindeer changes every year for the first seven years of its life. Another important element of the language is its abundance of expressions for describing relationships within the

K*

family, underlining the importance of family life among Lapp communities.

As Professor Erkki Asp points out in a study of the significance of Lappish in Lapp society, the role of the language is twofold; in the first place it serves as a means of communication and secondly it is a symbol. As Lappish is probably the key to the Lapps' survival as a distinct people, there is considerable concern among interested groups that its use should be encouraged. As already mentioned, a number of factors work against Lappish, and in all three of the Nordic countries the number of those who speak Lappish is declining all the time. It is interesting that a large number of those Lapps living in Inari interviewed for Asp's investigations had changed their first language from Lappish to Finnish—44 per cent said that although they had learnt Lappish first they regarded Finnish as their main language, while a further 16 per cent spoke as much Finnish as Lappish every day. Asp also refers to an inquiry conducted by Knut Kolsrud in Norway, which showed that the larger the Lapp majority in a commune, the better they resisted 'Norwegianisation', and says that the same holds true for Finland. The communes of Kautokeino and Karasjok in Norway, and Utsjoki in Finland, all of which have Lapp majorities, resist outside pressures more successfully than those places with only a few Lappish-speakers.

The question of language has always attracted considerable attention at the triennial meetings of the Nordic Lapp Council, held to discuss Lapp problems. At the first meeting in 1953, for example, Professor Erkki Itkonen proposed that a committee should be established to consider how about a thousand urgently needed 'culture words' could be introduced into Lappish. While Lappish is well-developed grammatically, there are certain difficulties, such as the lack of a standard orthography, which must be overcome before it can be successfully used as a literary language.

Although the word 'Lapp' is used in English, Swedish and a number of other languages (cf Finnish: *lappalainen*), the Lapps prefer to call themselves *samek* or *sabmelaẑẑak* (singular: *sabme, sabmelaš*). The Norwegians have always referred to the Lapps as *Finner*, though in Swedish this means 'Finns'. Nowadays many Norwegians and Swedes use *samer* (singular: *same*), the Finnish version of which is *saamelaiset* (singular: *saamelainen*).

HOW THEY LEARN

One of the most important institutions as far as the survival of Lappish is concerned is the school, which can stimulate an interest in the language by using it as a means of instruction or kill it by concentrating on the majority language. One of the main points of dispute has been whether the Lapps should have their own schools, such as, for example, the Swedish *nomadskola* (nomad school), a number of which existed for children who accompanied their parents on the long migrations, or whether Lapp children should attend the same schools as others. While special schools might be able to pay more attention to the Lapp children's problems, they might also increase their isolation, making them feel different and so inferior. Some people say that the nomad schools did exactly this.

Sweden now has Lapp schools to which Lapps can send their children if they wish, and these are in many ways comparable with the standard Swedish comprehensive school. They give a nine-year course, and although the teaching language is Swedish particular attention is paid to the study of the Lapp language and culture. In many Norwegian primary schools in the Lapp area children are at first taught in Lappish, while Norwegian is treated as the first foreign language, and measures are being taken to provide more education in Lappish at later stages. The Finnish Ministry of Education set up a committee to study the educational needs of Lapp children in the light of the new school system, and in autumn 1971 it recommended that Lapp children should be taught in their mother tongue for at least the first two years of the comprehensive school. In the past Lapps in all three countries have suffered from a shortage of Lappish-speaking teachers and textbooks in Lappish. Recently, following pressure from interested groups and a more favourable attitude from the authorities, matters have begun to improve.

The Lapps still have little or no chance of pursuing higher education in their own language, however, and the number of Lapp pupils taking the school-leaving examinations appears to be rather low. Whether too many of them simply drop out before they reach this stage, or whether by the time they approach the final examination they have become so well integrated with the majority culture that they no longer appear to be Lapps, is not clear. So far few Lapps seem to have attained professional or managerial positions, though this is changing as more qualify as doctors and teachers, for example, while an increasing number of Lapp girls are training to be nurses. Lappish courses are available in a number of universities in the Nordic countries, while in some there are departments concentrating on Lapp studies in the widest sense.

At the time of the Russian revolution in 1917 there were only three primary schools in the whole of the Kola peninsula. Since that time the situation has improved greatly and now all the Lapps living in the Soviet Union are considered to be literate. There has been a considerable demand for teachers, and since 1949 training for Kola Lapps has been provided by the Herzen Institute in Leningrad.

PRESS AND RADIO

As most Lapps are at least bilingual they are able to take advantage of the mass media available to the majority population. Also, in addition to newspapers and magazines and radio and television broadcasts in Swedish, Norwegian and Finnish, there are a number of publications in Lapp, while each country provides several hours of Lapp language broadcasting a week.

In 1898 the Free Church in Norway began publication of a paper for the Lapps in Lappish, called *Nuorttanaste*, and this is still available today. *Sagat*, which is in both Norwegian and

Lappish, was established in 1956 and has since become the leading organ of the Lapps in Norway. In Sweden there is a paper called *Samefolket*, which is mainly in Swedish with a few Lapp articles. *Samefolket* first appeared in 1919. The Society for the Promotion of Lapp Culture (Lapin Sivistysseura) and the Association of Finnish Lapps (Samii Litto) publish a paper, *Sabmelaš*, which has eight issues a year and is distributed free to all Lapp families in Finland.

LAPP ORGANISATIONS

The future of the Lapps may be somewhat uncertain, but public interest in them and their problems has never been greater than it is at present. To a certain extent this is due to the activities of the Lapps themselves; feeling their position to be in danger, and inspired by the struggle of other minorities, they have started to make their voices heard. Throughout history the Lapps seem to have adopted a fatalistic attitude when under pressure from outsiders; in most cases it was easier to move than resist, and this, coupled with the generally unsettled nature of their way of life, has militated against the formation of any form of self-government or administration. So too has the vastness of the area over which the tiny Lapp population was spread, and the fact that this area stretched over several countries which were not always on the best of terms. Until relatively recently the horizons of the average Lapp were bounded by the needs of his family and immediate community; he would only rarely come into contact with outsiders, apart from casual meetings on the trail or at the autumn and spring round-up. During the present century, however, with the development of communications and the tendency towards settled living a number of associations have been formed to safeguard Lapp interests.

In 1904 an organisation to represent the Lapps of Sweden was founded at Vilhelmina, and out of this grew the Central Union of Lapps in 1918, though lack of interest among the

Lapps and the negative attitude of the Swedish authorities led to the Union's collapse in 1923. During the 1930s and the 1940s the attitudes of the government changed and in 1950 the National Union of Swedish Lapps—Svenska Samernas Riksförbund—was formed to protect the rights of Lapps in Sweden. The Society for the Promotion of Lapp Culture—Lapin Sivistysseura—was founded in Helsinki in 1932, while in 1945 the Lapps formed their own organisation, the Association of Finnish Lapps—Samii Litto. In September 1971 a proposal was put forward to form a new association, in spite of opposition from Samii Litto. Area associations for the Norwegian Lapps were founded in the first decade of the present century, and in 1948 the Norwegian Reindeer Lapps Association—Norges Reindriftssamers Landsforening—and Sámiid Saervi—which in 1951 became Sámi Saervi-Samisk Selskap (The Lapp Association)—were founded.

The need for an inter-Nordic approach to Lapp problems had been recognised for some time when in 1953 delegates from many of the Lapp organisations arranged an international meeting at Jokkmokk in Sweden. A proposal that a Nordic Lapp Council should be established was accepted. The Jokkmokk conference was the first of the regular gatherings that have been held at three-yearly intervals to discuss Lapp affairs. A wide range of topics are discussed, including reindeer-breeding, education, language and Lapp culture in general, and recommendations are frequently passed on to the national governments and the Nordic Council.

THE POSITION OF THE LAPPS AND LAPLAND

It has been pointed out that the province of Lappi is a backward area when compared with the rest of the country. Indeed one Finnish politician has commented that if the drift to the south continues, Finnish Lapland will be empty before the end of the present century. In Finnmark the situation is similar, but in Sweden the presence of mineral reserves in the Kiruna area (in particular the famous 'Iron Mountain') has made the picture less bleak economically. However the establishment of new industries has created problems of another kind. There is a certain paradox about the position of Lapland at the present time; on the one hand the area is in desperate need of new industries and sources of power, while on the other it is very often the provision of these that endangers the old way of life. For example Kiruna, which lies some seventy miles north of the Arctic Circle, produces some of the richest iron ore in the world. Not surprisingly its exploitation has attracted a large work force from the south, and has also given work to people from all over the Lapland area, Finns and Norwegians as well as Swedes. At the same time the expansion of mining brings pollution and a threat to the environment. Workers from Kiruna and other industrial plants build summer cottages on the banks of rivers and lakes and use these as bases for fishing and hunting expeditions, killing for sport the fish, birds and animals on which some of the Lapps rely for a living. The high wages paid to labourers, truck-drivers and other workers at the industrial plants attract young Lapps away from their own culture, and many of the older generation are afraid that they will never return.

In many places the need for power has meant that hydro-electric stations have been built. These not only block the water-courses, restricting the use of rivers for transportation purposes, but in a number of places reservoirs have been constructed which drown land on which the Lapps used to graze reindeer and other animals.

For some the future of 'the last great wilderness in Europe' lies in tourism, but there are many who feel that this would not be a positive development. The tourist brings a pollution of his own with his cars and caravans and demand for hotels, guest houses and entertainment. Reindeer-herders see cars as a danger to their animals, while many Lapps are afraid that a large increase in the tourist trade will turn them into 'camera fodder'. Here, too, a paradox can be seen, for tourists mean new roads and improved services, settlements that were previously isolated are being brought into contact with the outside world, and road-building and maintenance and improved communications in general mean new jobs.

The threat to the Lapps' position is a real one. Although many Lapps have retained their language and other elements of their culture, there are many forces working against them. Farming, supplemented by hunting, fishing and forestry, as practised by many Lapps, can never be a particularly profitable occupation in the harsh conditions of Lapland, and there are few alternatives. While reindeer-breeding provides a reasonably good livelihood, few Lapps are in fact engaged in this today, and there appears to be little prospect of the numbers increasing. Faced with the realities of gaining a living it seems likely that an increasing number of Lapps will try to find work among the members of the majority community, either in Lapland or elsewhere, which will lead to a weakening of Lapp ties.

Nevertheless in many ways the future of the Lapps as a distinct people seems brighter today than for many years. In spite of the difficulties, such as those outlined in this chapter, the authorities in national and provincial capitals are realising that the Lapps have legitimate interests and that their opinions must be respected. A great deal was made of a recent Lapp suggestion that the question of the Lapp language in Finland should be taken to the United Nations, the issue being discussed at considerable length in the press and elsewhere. The Lapps of Sweden have a special *ombudsman* to look after their interests and it has been suggested that a similar official should be appointed in Finland too.

It is interesting too that a number of young Lapps are taking an interest in Lapp problems. Typical of these is Nils-Aslak Valkeapää, who has done much to revive the *juoigo* (the traditional chant song of the Lapps) and bring the problems of the Lapps before a wider audience. At least the Lapps' future will not go by default as seemed to be a possibility earlier this century.

IO

Hints for Visitors

FOR many people Finland seems remote, but there are excellent land, sea and air connections with other parts of Europe and also further afield. London to Helsinki takes three hours by a BEA or Finnair jet, while a plane leaving Helsinki at 10.30 am arrives in New York at 5.05 pm the same day. The Russian Baltic Steamship Company operates a service between London and Leningrad which calls at Helsinki, while there are also connections between Helsinki, Turku and other Finnish ports, and West Germany, Denmark and Sweden. Virtually all these routes, operated by companies such as Silja, Finnlines and Viking, provide regular sailings on fast, comfortable, purpose-built car ferries at reasonable prices. Land connections include the rail-link between Finland and the Soviet Union (there is also a comparatively little used road-link) and the roads between Finland and her Nordic neighbours north of the Gulf of Bothnia.

There are good air, train and bus services operating throughout the country. It is advisable to reserve seats on *pikajunat* (express trains) in advance, particularly during holiday periods. The reservation ticket should be retained, as often there is no indication that a place has been reserved on the seat itself. The same applies to long-distance buses, and the intending passenger should check with the conductress to see which places are still vacant in order to minimise the risk of ejection when additional passengers get on.

Although many of the roads in Finland are of indifferent quality, the private car is by far the best way to see the country.

Filling stations are plentiful, at least on major highways; a wide range of petrol brands are available. Finnish drivers tend to be reckless, and the pedestrian is regarded as a traffic hazard with few if any rights. The foreign driver is often surprised to see that many Finns drive with their car lights on during the daytime in both winter and summer, a practice that is officially encouraged as it makes vehicles easier to see.

There are a variety of facilities available for the tourist, ranging from camping sites and wilderness huts to hotels of different standards and prices. The *matkailijakoti* (traveller's home) will provide plain but generally comfortable accommodation for about £1.90 ($4.65) a person, while a room for one at a *motelli* would be approximately £2.80 ($6.86). The prices of hotel rooms vary according to the class of hotel, but start at about £3 ($7.35) in towns, rising to £6 ($14.70) or more. There is no charge for the use of wilderness huts, which are, as their name suggests, usually found in deserted places, but the person who spends a night there is expected to leave the place tidy and cut some wood ready for the next wayfarer. The standard of camping sites is generally high, and there are a number of youth hostels. During the summer months many student hostels are turned into *kesähotellit* (summer hotels) which provide reasonably cheap rooms for tourists.

As we have seen in the chapter on 'How They Live', many foodshops are run on self-service lines, so obviating the need to learn the Finnish names for items of food and drink. It is doubtful whether many holiday-makers will have either the time or inclination to learn Finnish, but they will usually find few language difficulties. Virtually all educated Finns know at least one foreign language (in addition to Finnish and Swedish), while some have learnt two or three. The Finns have appreciated that, as few people outside Finland want to learn Finnish, if they wish to communicate with the outside world they must learn foreign languages. A large part (some say too large a part) of the school curriculum is devoted to studying English and German, while French and Russian are also quite widely taught in addition to the two national languages. Owing to the stress most Finnish teachers put on grammar, many Finns are self-conscious about speaking foreign languages for fear they make mistakes, but in fact their standard of pronunciation and degree of fluency is usually good, particularly among the younger generation.

There is still considerable formality in Finnish social life and the foreigner has to be on guard in case he inadvertently commits a social blunder. When meeting someone for the first time it is customary to shake hands, at the same time giving one's name. On subsequent occasions, or if one is introduced by a third person, the customary greeting is '*Hyvää päivää*' (literally 'Good-day'), which is frequently shortened to '*Päivää*', colloquially. Like French, German, Swedish and some other languages, Finnish has a formal and informal 'you' form, the second person singular *sinä* being reserved for friends and relatives and the second person plural *te* for other people. Among older people, and some younger ones too, it is considered extremely impolite to address somebody using the *sinä* form unless a mutual agreement to do so has been made: this takes the form of the woman, or in the case of two men the senior of the two, suggesting that 'the titles should be dropped', which means that from henceforward the *sinä* form and first names will be used. Many Finns also have a high regard for titles, and in addition to academic titles, such as *maisteri* (which means much the same as an Oxbridge MA, but is used before a name, eg Maisteri Salmi) and *tohtori* (Doctor), there are also professional titles such as *varatuomari* (a lawyer) and *insinööri* (an engineer), both of which mean that their holder has taken a formal qualification, and occupational titles that go with a particular position, for example *pankinjohtaja* (bank manager) and *lehtori* (lecturer or senior teacher). Honorary titles such as *kauppaneuvos* (commercial counsellor) and *teollisuusneuvos* (industrial counsellor) are purchased for their holders as a mark of respect by the institution or company to which they belong.

Visitors to Finland may also find the following information useful. Shops usually open at 9 am and close at 5 pm though some large stores stay open later, particularly in summer;

Saturday closing times are 2 or 3 pm in most cases. It is worth remembering that most self-service foodshops give free plastic bags with the purchases (which are useful later for disposing of rubbish). Banks are open between 9.15 am and 4.30 pm, and are closed on Saturdays. It is virtually impossible for a mere customer to work out the licensing laws or regulations governing drinking, which are laid down by Alko and vary according to the class of restaurant or bar. Smoking is not permitted in buses, cinemas or theatres and is frowned upon in shops. Finally, particularly important for those with small children, there is an acute shortage of public lavatories in Finland, especially in towns. Those that do exist charge about 4p (9 cents) often for very indifferent facilities. It seems strange that a country which pays considerable attention to the welfare and comfort of people should neglect to supply such an elementary service, but presumably there is a fear that if public lavatories are freely available they would become the rendezvous of drunks and other undesirables. However, on the credit side most garages and cafés provide free toilets for customers, and these should be taken advantage of whenever possible.

Acknowledgements

I AM very grateful to the many people who have assisted me during the preparation of this book. In particular I should like to thank Professor Erkki Asp, Mr Bo Lundell, Dr George Maude, Dr Eeva Kangasmaa-Minn, Dr Karl Nickul, Mr Teuvo Tikkanen and his colleagues at Finnfacts, and Mr Reino Vahersaari, all of whom have generously put their time and knowledge at my disposal.

My greatest debt is to my wife Merja who, despite preoccupations of her own, cheerfully acted as secretary, research assistant and critic, and without whom this book could not have been written.

Index